A MOTHER'S REFLECTIONS

A MOTHER'S REFLECTIONS

A Heartwarming Journey of Love, Unyielding Strength, and Championing Inclusivity

DR SHANTI AULUCK

HAY HOUSE

HAY HOUSE INDIA
New Delhi • London • Sydney
Carlsbad, California • New York City

Hay House Publishers (India) Pvt Ltd,
Muskaan Complex, Plot No. 3, B-2, Vasant Kunj, New Delhi 110 070, India

Hay House LLC, P.O. Box 5100, Carlsbad, CA 92018-5100, USA
Hay House UK Ltd, 1st Floor, Crawford Corner, 91-93 Baker Street, London W1U 6QQ, UK
Hay House Australia Publishing Pty Ltd, 18/36 Ralph St., Alexandria NSW 2015, Australia

Email: contact@hayhouse.co.in
Website: www.hayhouse.co.in

First published by Hay House India, 2024
Reprint, 2026
11 10 9 8 7 6 5 4 3 2

ISBN 978-81-19554-66-9
ISBN 978-81-19554-48-5 (Ebook)

Printed at Repro India Limited

FSC
www.fsc.org
MIX
Paper from responsible sources
FSC® C047271

Hay House is committed to a sustainable future for our business, our readers and our planet. This book is made from Forest Stewardship Council® certified paper.

This book is dedicated to my dear son Puneet, a great teacher in my life, who inspired me to write this book. And to all those with intellectual and developmental disabilities whose presence in our lives teaches us lessons in humanism and inclusivity.

Contents

III

THE LONG ROAD AHEAD: CHANGING HEARTS AND MINDS IN DISABILITY DISCOURSE

Preface

I have tried to capture the internal odyssey within the book, which gained significant momentum with the unfolding of life's pivotal moments. Everything was going well until my second child arrived. Today, I feel as though my child had to teach me some important lessons in life that were essential for delving into intense existential inquiries that emerged within me at an early age. The inner child in me sought to 'see' God, leading to increasingly complex questions with no easy answers. The birth of my second child, a son with Down Syndrome, proved to be a shattering event for me, someone with a deep intellectual orientation of mind. This occurrence prompted numerous questions, not only challenging my own beliefs but also societal norms. The internal turmoil sparked unconventional thoughts that questioned conditioned perspectives on individuals, life, and the world at large.

This book encapsulates a wealth of diverse knowledge gleaned from the unique journey spurred by my son, Puneet. He presented me with intense moments of self-reflection, opportunities to apply my learnings to address the challenges, and a glimpse into the world of disabilities that often lingers at the periphery of our consciousness. It is different to see it from a distance than being in it. It feels as if each of the three sections of this book reflect my own development in life. These aspects of my personality were mutually reinforcing each other. I could become a nurturing mother because I could see follies in my thought process that created barriers in accepting my son with his disability. This insight was deepened as I understood how the mind functions, and that brought deep empathy within. It did not allow me to limit my concerns only for my child but many others who were living with such a condition, not because of their fault but because others were unfair to them due to biased perceptions, denying them basic human rights and growth opportunities.

Anything happening to a child is also happening to the mother. In the case of any disabling condition, one recognises that it is not a temporary phenomenon. Each aspect of one's life is affected by it, and a mother's heart cannot rest until she does everything possible to protect the child from adverse consequences and enrich her child's life.

The vast experiences mentioned above sparked a triple revolution within me. I became a mother struggling with my own emotions, a mother and a psychologist who was fully immersed in exploring the world of my son with limited intellectual capacities, and an activist keenly aware of the social injustice instrumental in impoverishing the lives of many individuals with disabilities. Something needed to be done to deal with the unrest within me, arising from the threefold aspects of my experiences. I not only tried to do whatever could be done with my son and many other individuals in similar conditions, but I was also intensely engaged in exploring the nature of mind functions.

These experiences have culminated in my writings encompassing three realms—reflections on my role as a mother, insights as a psychologist navigating the impact of intellectual disability on development, and advocacy work as an activist fuelled by a profound awareness of social injustice.

The mother in me was guided by a search for existential questions, the psychologist in me was trying to apply knowledge of human development and psychology to nurture and maximise the growth processes of Puneet, and the activist in me was inspired by myriad real-life heroes, friends with disabilities, who were working incessantly to carve out a path for themselves, facing all kinds of impediments in living a full life. They were leading the disability movement in India that will perhaps change the living conditions of generations of people with diverse forms of disabilities.

I
An Emotional Odyssey: Navigating Life with a Child with Down Syndrome

In this section, through a sequence of experiences, the readers will delve into the emotional odyssey of a mother who discovers that her son has Down Syndrome just forty-eight hours after his birth. It vividly portrays an inward journey characterised by the tumultuous interplay of love, grief, and despair. These emotions lay bare the profound impact societal norms have on our perceptions and emotional responses. As the narrative unfolds, it invites readers to question their own interpretations and judgments, paving the way for a transformative exploration of self and others.

This part also examines the world we construct through our perceptions and judgment tendencies. In this exploration, we encounter a vast and diverse universe awaiting our discovery, offering opportunities to broaden our perspectives on life and self. The narrative underscores the potential for embracing and respecting the multitude of ways people navigate their existence.

Growing alongside my son Puneet, I gradually recognised the simplicity of my previous world view, steeped in uniformity and certainty, as if only a handful of valid ways defined life. Much like a black hole conceals its own realities, each individual carries a universe within, with unique ways of experiencing life and the cosmos. A chapter in this section also captures the revelations gleaned from closely observing his feelings, needs, and behaviours. It demystifies the perplexity often felt in the presence of a person with intellectual disabilities (ID), emphasising that the fundamental essence of humanity, with its shared feelings and aspirations, remains constant, regardless of individual personalities.

The narrative acknowledges the substantial challenges that the presence of a person with ID poses to families. The last chapter explores the amplified difficulties faced by family members due to the absence of knowledge, guidance, and support services. This journey aims to illuminate the human experiences shared across diverse universes and foster a deeper understanding of the intrinsic worth of each individual, regardless of their unique path in the world.

1

A Mother's Journey

Life is a vast canvas of pleasures and pain, hopes and despair, success and failure, dreams, and aspirations. It is full of wonders and mysteries. From the tiniest atom to large galaxies, everything works in perfect order. Life itself appears to be an enigma, though we live with confidence and certainty as if we know and can control it. The falsity of this notion strikes us when we face difficult situations. Life has its own dynamism and follows its usual course unless one finds oneself in entirely unknown terrain brought about by unexpected events. It can sometimes change the entire course of life. What initially started as a shocking event may open up a completely new dimension of experience. Life teaches much more by putting us through struggles and suffering, provided we do not succumb to them. I sometimes wonder if I could know life as closely if Puneet was not there in my life. It proved to be a turning point in my life in many ways.

Back in April 1976, I was to become the mother of my second child. I had a six-year-old daughter who was a delight to us—my husband, her grandparents, and me—in every way. Having just completed my PhD in Psychology, I decided to take a break in my career so that I could look after my baby well and enjoy his growing-up period. Everything was going well in life, and I felt blessed to have a caring husband and a delightful daughter. The time for delivery came, and I didn't have the faintest apprehension about anything going wrong. We were overjoyed to have a son, but the joy was short-lived. Two days after his birth, the doctor told us that he had Down's Syndrome and that such children do not fully develop in their intellectual ability. I was shocked and started looking for all the signs and symptoms to falsify the doctor's diagnosis. The diagnosis was catastrophic, plunging me into denial and disbelief. Desperate to disprove the diagnosis, I scrutinised every aspect of my child.

I remained in a state of denial for days, though with an apprehension about what if the diagnosis was true. Soon began a period of intense grief. I could visualise how our life was going to be affected by it. It was the most severe blow for a person like me for whom intellect meant so much. Denial, however, could not bring me peace because the faintest possibility of the diagnosis being true was too horrifying. I went through the process of confirmations and reconfirmations, forcing myself to confront reality squarely within days of Puneet's birth. I did not cry; it felt as if everything within me had dried up, and life was over in every conceivable way. Intense and unrelenting grief took over me, and sleep became a refuge. The reality was so frightening that I did not want to discuss it with anyone, including my husband, as it would have reminded me of the situation that I desperately wanted to forget. I lived with a strange feeling of derealisation and depersonalisation, part of a post-traumatic psychological condition.

My son, Puneet, is now 47 years old. He is a caring and responsible member of our family, spreading love and happiness with his zestful and endearing ways. Reflecting on his growth from childhood, I never imagined that he would grow up to be such a pleasant, mature, and wonderful person. Watching him grow has shattered various myths about intellectual disability, providing me with a rare opportunity to explore and understand emotional, personality, and cognitive aspects in someone with limited intellectual abilities.

Daily interactions with Puneet have sparked numerous interesting questions about the workings of the human mind. These questions presented a fascinating challenge to my quest for understanding the mind more deeply. It has great potential for psychological research, revealing deeper mysteries of the mental processes. While tempted to pursue this as a research area, my maternal instincts prevailed in shaping the direction of my life. Like any mother, I yearned for Puneet to have the best opportunities for a happy life, though the journey to secure them was far from easy. Challenges such as a lack of good educational opportunities and prevailing misconceptions in society became significant hurdles. It's disheartening to see how societal misconceptions—whether based on caste, gender, or disability, can impoverish lives.

Persons with ID often face underestimation, hindering their access to essential opportunities like education, skill training, and employment. Under these circumstances, creating proper conditions for Puneet's development meant taking matters into my own hands. I connected with like-minded parents embarking on a collective effort to find solutions for the lack of services in this field. It gave birth to Muskaan, an NGO in Delhi, run by parents and professionals, focused on securing the basic human rights of children and adults with ID.

Ironically, Puneet was born a month after I submitted my PhD thesis in Psychology, marking it as an intense period of intellectual engagement. Amidst despair, two conflicting thoughts were emerging in my mind. On one hand, there was an utter disappointment of having a child with an intellectual disability; on the other hand, the call for duty was emerging, reminding me of my responsibility as a mother to nurture Puneet's growth so that he could actualize his fullest potential. While navigating conflicting emotions, I also realised that my grief was a kind of insult to his existence—a new life that had every right to enjoy this wonderful world and its beauty in his own ways.

A Mother's Reflections: An Inward Journey

In the years since Puneet's birth, I have been on an intensive inward journey, wherein life has been providing me with profound insights into myself, the human nature, and life in general. This transformative path, laden with diverse challenges, was anything but easy. The struggles, primarily internal, stirred me to the core.

Sometimes, I wonder how significant transformations can occur when we question ourselves, others, and the situations that life presents to us. A child who initially brought immense grief and despair into my life has now become the greatest blessing. His simple and innocent ways, purity of heart, capacity for love and cheer, freedom from egocentric persuasions, and zest for life are truly touching. I cherish a beautiful relationship with him, born out of total unconditional love and acceptance for both him and his condition. This journey has enabled me to experience the profound beauty of unconditional love, offering a unique and diverse understanding of life.

Was this transformation easy and quick? Absolutely not! It required years of churning before reaching the present state of mind. There were moments in early days when I wished he hadn't survived, contemplating placing him in an institution to protect our lives. Strangely, these reactions came from someone who saw herself as a kind-hearted and sensitive person, who was deeply touched by other's difficulties and sufferings. Despite these negative feelings, my care for my innocent child never wavered, although I occasionally unleashed my anger on him during his childhood, always followed by strong feelings of guilt.

Coping with the new realities of life presented a huge challenge. It meant questioning my beliefs, prejudiced notions, my intellectual snobbishness, and judgmental attitudes. However, my inclination to search for answers within myself led to introspection, self-analysis, and struggles with my own self. This proved to be revealing in terms of insights about my own self, highlighting unhealthy attitudes and egocentric ways of thinking at the root of my problems. I could clearly see a symbiotic connection that a mother shares with her children. Children are such a significant part of their parents that they become almost like an extension of them. Just as we feel pain, shame, anger, and frustration at any kind of damage to our image, the failures and pains of our children become our loss as well. Similarly, their achievements give us great pride and happiness. My introspective analysis revealed this to be an important source of my troubles and I realised the need for bringing objectivity in my approach. The fact is that children have to face their own difficulties, deprivations, and failures. We, as parents, can only support and encourage them in their journey.

Fulfilling our aspirations through children is not fair. Each of us is born with a script that unfolds as we grow up. Our own dispositions and circumstances create a certain field of action, defining our roles and duties. There is no guarantee that life's outcomes will align with our expectations. When we choose to be parents, we have no way of influencing the kind of person our child will become. We cannot choose their abilities, constitution, or any other qualities. A child with a disability is the least we might expect. However, it is unfair for parents to place unrealistic expectations on their children. Parenting is about helping them grow and develop according to their abilities and dispositions, so that they become optimally functional and wholesome individuals. The key to our happiness should lie within us, and we should not blame our circumstances or others because they cannot always be conducive to our sense of well-being. A famous *sloka* from the Bhagavad Gita serves as an important reminder: '*karmanyev adhikaraste, ma phaleshu kadachana* [We can only perform actions to the best of our ability and understanding, but the results are not entirely in our hands].'

Self-images or notions about ourselves are at the root of our self-esteem, playing a vital role in creating a sense of well-being and self-confidence. Our happiness or unhappiness depends mostly on experiences that enhance our self-image or dent it. This profound insight into the human mind is well captured in Brihadaranyaka Upanishad Chapter IV, Volume 6: '*Atmanastu kamay sarvam priyam bhawati* [It is for the love of self that all is loved].'

The noted Buddhist monk Gyatso once said: 'All the fearful aspects of Samasara, from the greatest down to the smallest, arise from the self-cherishing attitude.'

I came to realise that the roots of my grief and sadness lay in the dents suffered by me at the thought that my child would not develop normally. Deficiency in intelligence would impact his behaviour in ways that were unacceptable to me. I needed to work on such thoughts and be more realistic and objective.

My introspective analysis revealed another troubling area. I had always valued intellectual orientation, almost bordering on intellectual snobbishness. My own child having an intellectual disability was too upsetting and painful. However, a rational and philosophical view helped me notice the faults in my thinking. I started seeing my grief as an unfair reaction. I realised how unfair it was to a value judgement on someone's life. Deep down, I saw the working of a utilitarian perspective that was obstructing me from accepting him as he was. As I moved on with such thoughts, I realised the narrowness of utilitarian attitudes that we as humans often hold. It gradually resulted in the development of deep reverence within me for all forms of diversity in people as well as all creations in nature.

Many of my apprehensions were arising from the social stigma attached to intellectual disability and the consequent social embarrassment. I could visualise people's reactions to my son and the inherent embarrassment in such situations. I was also pained at the thought that my daughter would have to go through emotional difficulties due to her brother being 'non-normal'. Surprisingly, at that time, it did not occur to me that my son, Puneet, too, could have emotional difficulties. Perhaps, I assumed that he would not be able to know and experience such problems. I realised later that it was a false presumption. Persons with intellectual disabilities have the capacity for self-awareness as well as experience the whole range of emotions like any other person. Such false presumptions from others become roadblocks in their fuller development. It gradually dawned on me that the solution lay in accepting the reality of my son's condition and fighting with my own hypocrisy, faulty notions, and attitudes. The two-fold challenge, i.e., helping him grow as fully as possible and working on my own attitudes, brought deep inner transformation in my ways of thinking and being. I see him today as the most precious person in my life who taught me valuable lessons and gave me rich insights into human psychology. He taught me the true meaning of unconditional love.

Wonderful Experiences of Being a Mother

Bringing up my son has been a profoundly enriching experience. Drawing on my background in psychology helped me identify areas of development that needed special efforts at different stages of his upbringing. I recognised the importance of wider exposure, simple daily tasks that foster motor coordination, self-management skills, appropriate social behaviour, language acquisition, conceptual development, self-awareness, and above all, self-esteem and emotional security.

There were several instances that revealed Puneet's comprehension extending beyond our presumptions. One day, while he was alone watching TV, at the age of 15, I asked him about the programme. His response '*mere jaise bacchon ka programme hai*' [It is a programme about children like myself]'. This statement was an eye-opener for me regarding his capacity for self-awareness and understanding of the differences between himself and others.

Another striking incident occurred when his sister got married and moved to the USA. After bidding her farewell at the airport and returning home late in the night, I overheard him in her room, kissing her photos and saying, '*Main ab akela ho gaya hoon*' (I am now alone].' Hearing him say this made me cry. It was a moment of revelation of his feelings and sentiments. He was 20 years old then.

It is unjust when we underestimate the humanness of a person with ID. Puneet's unique needs became focal points in our interactions with him. Parenting him wasn't fundamentally different from raising other children, except that we made a conscious effort to create tailored learning experiences for him. Recognising the importance of motivational factors in his learning, we often employed innovative and creative teaching methods. Learning sessions were always made enjoyable with lots of hugs and appreciation. Playing ludo and building with Lego blocks provided opportunities to teach him concepts of size, colour, shapes, and constructive play. Similarly, activities like ball throwing, badminton, and cricket required various types of motor coordination. All these activities were accompanied by a great deal of verbal communication, enhancing his awareness of various objects and surroundings, including stimulation for language development. He was introduced to drawing and colouring at the age of 3–4 years, which helped build his attention, concepts and fine motor coordination as well as the development of a hobby. He has remained engaged with this hobby, creating complex and fine designs. Every task that he engaged with gave him an opportunity for accomplishment which boosted his confidence and self-esteem, critical to a sense of emotional well-being.

My family played an important role in his development. My husband and daughter have always been extremely gentle and supportive towards him. My daughter served as a role model for Puneet, making me aware of his needs as an adolescent and securing his rights, which I sometimes overlooked due to my own preoccupations. She acted as both a companion and nurturant adult. We never burdened her with unfair demands and expectations, allowing her to develop her own adaptations to the situations. We understood that parents can play a significant role in shaping the attitudes and behaviour of siblings, as well as of other relatives and friends, towards a person with a disability.

Placing myself in Puneet's position and understanding his world expanded my consciousness. It also helped in comprehending his emotional reactions and behaviour, fostering respect for his individuality. Intellectual disability in a person often tends to become such an overwhelming concern that people fail to notice other aspects of the person, and this perpetuates negative biases. It is interesting to note that emotions and personality of a person with ID follow a normal course of development as in others. Sexuality also unfolds at its usual age. Lack of its recognition and proper channelisation often brings resentment and disruptive behaviour in an individual. Intellectual impairment does not affect development in other areas of personality e.g. feelings, physical and psychological needs, aspirations, interests, and temperament. Psycho-social needs remain crucial, and healthy development hinges on self-esteem and emotional well-being.

Years of keen observation and introspection were required to reach my current state of mind. Each small step in this direction was rewarding, leading to increased strength and inner calmness. My spiritual orientation enabled me to see the situation in a larger context. It is noteworthy that the Chinese language uses the same pictorial character for the words 'crisis' and 'opportunity'—they are indeed connected. The crises in our lives prompt us to re-examine our thinking and allow new meanings to unfold. My world changed because of my dear son, proving to be an *agni pareeksha* that burned away unnecessary attitudes and notions. I find more reasons to be joyful and eternally grateful for the small gifts of life.

Puneet, my son, has imparted some of life's most valuable lesson, and I would like to share them:

- Happiness is attainable without conditions. Dwelling on what we lack can lead to significant losses in life.
- The essence of reverence is found in accepting and respecting all forms of creation—whether plants, animals, or humans. We are integral parts of a larger, mysterious order in the universe.
- Unconditional or selfless love is difficult to acquire, yet it enriches both the giver and the receiver. It establishes a precious connection where the well-being of others takes precedence. Cultivating selfless love fosters compassion as a natural response to the world.
- Embracing patience towards everyone cultivates an attitude that makes life easier and more peaceful. It proves invaluable in navigating through challenging situations.
- We often expend excessive energy in seeking personal glory, forgetting that it fulfils an emotional need for everyone. Building understanding and sensitivity towards others contributes to a more harmonious existence.

- Each sorrow possesses the potential to nurture maturity and strength. The key lies in examining how we respond to the challenges that life presents.
- Life is inherently simple and beautiful when we refrain from creating unnecessary complications.
- Celebrating simple joys adds a profound beauty to life.

2

My Son, Puneet

In this chapter, I delve into the life journey of my son Puneet, based on my recollections of observations spanning his growth from infancy to adulthood. At 47 years of age, Puneet's life story intertwines with my own, compelling me to confront my emotions and inner turmoil, ultimately resulting in a profound transformation. It brought about a shift in perspective and emotional calmness, allowing me to objectively view all kinds of challenges in life and focus on finding solutions rather than dwelling on problems.

Puneet provided me with opportunities to examine and question numerous misconceptions about judging people—a practice not only unfair but also a source of conflicts and unhappiness. I discovered that understanding his behaviours required nothing more than applying common human psychology, a skill most parents develop intuitively.

Fortuitously, I chose to perceive Puneet as an individual with his own needs, interests, and temperament, relegating his disability to a secondary consideration.

Though initially engulfed in grief over his condition, I resolved to dedicate all possible efforts to nurturing Puneet's fullest growth. Drawing on my education in psychology, I understood his developmental needs and took on the responsibility of teaching him various skills along with attending to his emotional well-being. Opting not to enlist caretakers or therapists, I guided his journey, a decision that has filled me with pride and satisfaction as Puneet blossomed into a mature, sensitive, and responsible adult, radiating love and cheer.

From an early age, Puneet displayed keen interest, zest, vivacity, and affection. Now, at 47 years old, he epitomises adulthood in every aspect—his emotions, behaviours, responses to situations, sense of responsibility, preferences, and expectations. A delightful presence at home, Puneet attentively listens, takes charge of his daily life, and revels in every moment without succumbing to aimless action and boredom. Disciplined and structured in his activities, he neither seeks nor expects concessions, remains free from unnecessary comparisons or competition, and embraces everyone with an open heart.

His life is characterised by a lack of anger or frustration. Puneet engages in hobbies such as drawing, painting, and music, and carefully selects programmes to watch on TV. Calm, happy, and affectionate, he cherishes relationships with cousins, uncles, aunts, neighbours, and friends, missing his sister who left home 28 years ago after marriage. Puneet vehemently rejects being treated as a child, asserting, 'I am not a child.' An obedient son who adapts to situations as needed, he rises to the occasion when required, cherishing his own space and freedom.

He went through various stages of development like any other boy of his age, exhibiting characteristic behaviours. He began schooling at the age of five. He joined Muskaan in 1995 at the age of 17 where he received vocational training. Later, he joined the supported employment centre of

Muskaan and worked in the stationary unit for almost 20 years. He preferred to work on paper products and enjoyed making gift bags and block printing on them. He was happy working on stationary products in Muskaan until an opportunity for mainstream employment came from Lemon Tree Hotels, Delhi. He, along with four other boys working in Muskaan, were picked up for training in the hospitality department of the hotel in 2014.

It was first time that a reputed hotel like Lemon Tree was opening its doors for the employment of individuals with Down Syndrome and other intellectual disabilities. I knew that Puneet would love it as he always enjoyed social interactions and making friends. He was a disciplined worker, thanks to his teachers at Muskaan who taught him good work ethics. After six months of hands-on training, he was hired as a guest associate in the food & beverages department. He was excited to receive a monthly salary of Rs 10,000, although its value is beyond his comprehension. He worked there for four years, following a hectic schedule of six working days with daily hours of 7 a.m. to 3 p.m. in the morning shift, or from 1 p.m. to 9 p.m. in the afternoon shift.

This demanding working schedule continued till he developed a spine problem in 2018. He showed remarkable resilience when he faced severe spine problems and had to undergo major spine surgery in January 2019. He remained calm, responsive to the health demands and its compliances. He was asked to refrain from certain movements to prevent the implants in his spine from being impacted. It was amazing to see him following all the dos and don'ts with utmost care. It was beyond my expectation; I saw a sense of self-responsibility in him for his well-being. I never had to worry that he may make some movements that may worsen his condition. He befriended the doctors, assistants, and surgeon, enjoying the camaraderie and sharing jokes with them. Puneet was a source of strength to me during this time. His adaptability to new situations, living in the 'now', love for work, a structured daily routine, and capacity for love and happiness gave me strength and reminded me what was truly important in life, rather than endless worries about small concerns of life.

During his illness, he once again took up the task of making gift bags from decorative paper. He diligently crafted gift bags at home every day, both before and after surgery, spanning over several months. The same structure and routine continued during the pandemic. He showed great discipline in his work and other daily activities. He rejoined the hotel in the winter of 2019 for part-time work. However, due to the pandemic, there was a two-year gap in his hotel employment, and he resumed working in the summer of 2022. He has no complaints in life—what a wonderful way to navigate the world!

Puneet has become a companion to me and my husband in our senior years. How has he grown to be what he is today? In retrospect, several insights come to my mind. Like everyone else, he has gone through all the psychological stages of life. His story encapsulates the universal experiences of infancy, childhood, adolescence, and adulthood, offering deep insights into the joys, challenges, and complexities of life that shape us all.

Puneet as an Infant

Puneet was not quite active in the initial two years of his life. He never ate properly and mostly survived on milk. He started teething late, which affected his ability to eat solids.

He started sitting at eight months, crawled on his belly when he was a year old, and suffered from frequent respiratory infections. He started walking when he was two-and-a-half-years old and spoke first word 'biscuit' when he was four. His activity levels increased with walking.

We consciously involved him in most activities, providing the necessary sensory stimulation for his growth. I played a dominant role in this process as I chose not to hire a caretaker. I wanted to participate in most daily activities with him, including play time. This decision gave me the opportunity to observe and understand his feelings and readiness for learning various self-help behaviours. We engaged in simple conversations during various activities to stimulate his language and speech comprehension—a preliminary step for language development. Giving hugs, appreciation, and playful interactions brought him immense joy and happiness, making it great fun to spend time with him. He took a huge interest in his surroundings and enjoyed our interactions with him.

His Childhood

Childhood is a stage of extensive learning and playful activities with peers. Children start learning social behaviours that prepare them to be responsible members of society. Children with intellectual disability are no different. However, a conscious effort needs to be made to help them learn the various dos and don'ts and other ways of the world. Puneet had a high level of activity that was often random in nature. Late teething created difficulties in chewing, which made him quite selective about his food, eating soft foods and drinking milk. All the nutrients were either mixed in milk or put in a parantha, which he relished.

He occasionally indulged in self-injurious behaviour like banging his head on the floor, spitting, and throwing things at visitors. Perhaps, he behaved in this manner to express his unhappiness or, at times, to force our attention towards him. I used these occasions to help him understand the undesirability of such behaviour. It had become a routine exercise whenever we had guests in our house. I was extra attentive towards him on such occasions so that he did not feel ignored. I was also careful about appreciating good behaviour. My dominant ways of dealing with negative behaviours were to engage him in constructive activities and explaining why certain behaviours were acceptable or unacceptable. Such conversations worked because he was internalising social values while constructive activities provided a boost to his self-esteem and self-image. Many negative behaviours arise from frustration and low self-esteem.

In his bid to enjoy his autonomy and freedom, he would often go out of the house, uninformed. As a result, we had to keep the main door of our house locked all the time. He showed stubbornness by not doing things that we asked him to do. However, I saw it as a form of self-assertion, a psychological need helping us to carve out our own identities—an important milestone in the development of the mind. It is built around the notion of our body and its functions, likes and dislikes, interests, pleasure and pain, feelings, emotions, others' reactions, etc. The designation of one's own space, clothes, items of personal utility, interactions with people and assignment of roles and responsibilities contribute to the formation of a simple self-identity. This process helps in the development of self-awareness, facilitating self-discipline, and self-regulation.

There is a common practice in every society to teach a child about their body, helping them identify different body parts—a crucial step in developing identity through association with body and 'me'. Asking the child about preferences or providing options to choose is an act of affirming the need for identity and self-expression. Dialogue is an effective way of building knowledge and awareness about oneself, others, and the physical and social environment. Such conversations should be carried on in a simple manner whenever the situation arises. Parents should not refrain from engaging in such interactions and conversations, worrying about whether the child can understand them or not. In fact, these conversations help in building receptive language, which is the foundation of understanding the world and language development.

Puneet's School Life

At the age of four, we enrolled Puneet in a nursery school. He attended various schools between the ages of 4 to 16 years. However, with the exception of the nursery school, all other schools failed to deliver quality education that could cater to the developmental needs of a child with ID. He joined Muskaan for vocational training at the age of 17. His schooling was never interrupted, even if there was no transport available. My husband and I took turns dropping off and picking him up.

At home, Puneet had his own space—a room with his own bed, table, chair, and cupboard. He enjoyed participating in various houschold activities such as washing utensils and folding clothes. Despite the mess and added work, I was patient with him, allowing him to engage in these activities. I believed that such activities would foster a sense of accomplishment that was essential for building self-confidence and initiative for new learning experiences. My effort was to create fun and learning situations where he could have successful experiences. It is important for self-esteem and plays a central role in psychological well-being. Additionally, these activities helped him develop sensory-motor skills and awareness of physical environment.

We engaged in a lot of conversations about matters important to his life. I played with him using various activities. My focus was to build his confidence and encourage him to play such games on his own during leisure time. He started using crayons for drawing and colouring, later progressing to colouring books, which he used extensively until the age of 30. I introduced him to picture books, explaining the stories. All my instructions, both dos and don'ts, were given in an explanatory manner, outlining the reasons behind them and how he would benefit. Initially, he used words to express himself, gradually progressing to two- or three-word sentences by the age of eight or nine years. Verbal communication played a dominant role, helping him in building his concepts, vocabulary, and analytical thinking. It provided him with a means of expression that contributed to emotional well-being.

Puneet as an Adolescent

This phase of development marked the dominance of social needs. Individuals acquire broader knowledge and learn skills essential for becoming responsible adults, gradually taking control of their lives. In Puneet's case, some earlier issues persisted, and new challenges emerged, such as fascination with girls, the emergence of sexuality, occasional flamboyance, negativity, bossiness, and the use of abusive words. However, I worked with him to channelise his energy and enthusiasm through engagement with interests and activities he liked. Puneet showed interest in music, dance, and theatre, participating in various workshops and classes. He enjoyed these activities and took part in several such activities in school and at Muskaan. He attended inclusive theatre workshops organised by the National School of Drama and renowned theatre director Barry John. He actively participated in dance events, attended Shiamak Dawar dance classes, and dance events at Muskaan and other public forums. He grew up as an energetic youth who enjoyed various pursuits.

My main focus was on helping him develop social and interpersonal skills. As he entered adolescence, our relationship gradually shifted from a typical mother-son dynamic to more of a friendship. Instead of dictating, I engaged in discussions, presenting options and encouraging him to make his own choices. This approach facilitated the development of his analytical thinking and instilled a sense of responsibility. Often, I would keep myself in his position and understand his feelings accordingly. It enhanced our mutual faith and trust. Puneet listened to me more and tried to follow what was being told to him, except for occasional lapses. He started becoming more and more sensitive to our needs and feelings along with better regulation of his own behaviour.

Young Adulthood

He started to stabilise between the ages of 22 and 25. Undesirable behaviours decreased, and there was a noticeable increase in sense of responsibility, along with taking charge of everyday life. Puneet exhibited enhanced self-awareness,

awareness of others and his environment, and a growing sense of self-discipline.

While interested in marriage, he understood its associated responsibilities as explained to him from time to time. He stopped insisting on it. He secured employment at the Supported Employment Centre of Muskaan and later at the Lemon Tree Hotel in Delhi. A diligent worker, Puneet approached his tasks with perfection, paying meticulous attention to details. Boredom did not find a place in his life, and I envied him for that.

He taught me to develop interaction styles that nurtured his growth and mine, too. I would like to share below a few thoughts that helped in nurturing Puneet's development and growth:

- I held a firm belief that human beings are inherently programmed for learning, giving me hope that efforts in teaching him would bear fruit. Schooling, I realised, wasn't solely about academic learning, which was especially challenging for him. Schools offer diverse learning situations, fostering discipline in formal social settings and exposure to various types of knowledge.
- Emphasis on the importance of self-reliance in daily activities, it enhances dignity, a sense of accomplishment, and overall well-being.
- Significance of building comprehension, self-awareness, and emotional-social understanding—these aspects became integral to my conversations and interactions with him.
- I examined my own faulty thinking that hindered unconditional acceptance of him and his condition.

- Overcoming the concern of 'what will people think?' gradually liberated me from the usual feeling of shame and embarrassment. I reminded myself that others' opinions were rooted in ignorance, and sharing knowledge about his condition was essential for facilitating proper understanding in others.
- A healthy family environment, marked by mutual understanding and emotional care, is necessary for every child, especially when one of the family members faced difficulties. Unnecessary manifestations of anxiety, anger, and frustration can disrupt the development of other children. Parents need to understand the difficulties of other children as well and avoid undue expectations.
- I recognised the importance of self-esteem and self-presentation in case of siblings, knowing that shame and embarrassment might adversely affect them. Maintaining harmony within the family and balanced behaviour by parents is crucial.
- It was clear to me that Puneet would gain a respectable place in the family, among friends and acquaintances only when we respected him. Immediate and extended family members—including grandparents, our daughter and her husband, our granddaughters, as well as both sides of our families—loved, cared for, valued, and respected Puneet. He has a cherished place in our entire circle of relatives and friends.
- Shifting from a parent-centric to a person-centric approach meant understanding his difficulties, world view, and feelings rather than focusing solely on our problems.

- I persisted with my efforts and perseverance without unrealistic expectations, never growing tired of it. I decided to continue working on his development, even if it meant repeating myself several times, recognising that repetitions formed the foundation of learning.
- Taking charge of training and teaching him various skills, such as daily needs, developing interests, instilling self-discipline, fostering appropriate social and emotional behaviour, encouraging language and communication, and building awareness about himself and his environment, became my responsibility. I chose not to hire a special educator or home-help for these tasks. It provided me with an opportunity to understand his reactions and behaviours. At the age of 10, Puneet had become quite independent in taking care of his daily needs.
- Throughout adolescence, I concentrated on his social and emotional behaviours. I transitioned from being his teacher to becoming more of a friend and mother, carrying a friendly dialogue most of the times.
- We acknowledged his sexuality without alarm, aiming to channelise it into more appropriate forms of expression and fulfilment.
- I didn't ignore any action or behaviour that I knew was not beneficial for him. I maintained unwavering faith in the learning capacity of every human being, regardless of disability, believing that he would grow up to be a responsive individual with appropriate interventions.
- As he grew older, I changed my interaction patterns. I engaged in conversations, explanations, and discussions about dos and don'ts, always explaining

the consequences of his actions and behaviours. I encouraged him to make his own decisions. Our mode of interaction focused on developing his awareness about himself, others, and social situations, maintaining a friendly atmosphere rather than a strictly parental one. Such an approach supported his growth in terms of emotional maturity, sense of responsibility, stability, and obedience.

- I was careful never to talk about him negatively in others' presence. If required, I used to highlight his positive qualities and behaviours when discussing him with others.
- It was important that my husband and I did not contradict each other while responding to Puneet. I took the charge of taking care of most of his needs while my husband supported my efforts. We always spoke separately if either of us found our interaction with Puneet unreasonable.
- I didn't want him to merely obey me. I actively sought occasions that encouraged his sense of responsibility, self-direction, and autonomy in personal matters, to the extent possible.
- Our mode of communication involved joking, talking about his needs, feelings, likes and dislikes, food preferences, and his favourite TV programmes, films, and actors. Our relationship was characterised by friendship.
- I never allowed him to use his disability as an excuse for any wrongdoing. Firm communication without harshness or anger was maintained.

- At times, I felt saddened by the deprivations in his life. During such moments, I analysed my feelings, realising the faults in my thinking. I accepted that everyone experiences their own pains and pleasures, including Puneet. As a family, our role is to support him when needed. Such objectivity in thinking needs to be embraced sooner or later with all our near and dear ones.
- It's never too late to learn and change; this applies to our intellectually challenged child as well, irrespective of age. Clarity, understanding, and determination is required for bringing a change.

Puneet as an Adult

Like everyone else, Puneet, now 47, has become matured, responsible, and is less reactive. He has become a companion for both me and my husband. To me, he is not merely a person with an intellectual disability; rather, his world fascinates me—it is simple and innocent, without any impurities or biases that we generally accumulate as we grow older. I wouldn't want him to be any different than he is.

I feel a certain kind of inner calm and freedom, as he has made me question many faulty beliefs, assumptions, prejudices, and worldly ways, enabling me to learn precious lessons from life. He has become a lighthouse in my life, guiding me through numerous situations. He is a great companion, and I am enjoying both his world and mine. As my initial inner turmoil settled, I became a more relaxed, calm, and peaceful person. He taught me styles of interpersonal interactions that nurtured his growth and mine as well. My interpersonal sensitivities, respect for differences, and nurturing attitude grew manifold.

Puneet turned out to be a blessing in my life, making it complete in many ways. He has taught me compassion, patience, perseverance, inner peace, gratitude, acceptance rather than judgment, empathy, and self-control. Above all, he has taught me how to live life, helping me see the beauty and joy in the small things of life.

As I reflect on Puneet, I believe it's beneficial for readers to understand how other siblings in the immediate and extended family observed and thought about him. Puneet has only one sister, six years older than him. My experience shows that a pleasant and normal home environment allows other children to grow well, fostering a loving and responsible attitude towards a sibling with intellectual difficulties.

Pallavi, Puneet's Sister

My first memory of Puneet is from when he was born. He was so tiny and fair, wrapped up in a black chenille shawl. I have no recollection of anyone telling me he was different in any way. Growing up, I was wrapped up in my own childhood and probably paid no mind to my younger brother except that he was sometimes an annoying sibling.

It was maybe when I was 9 years old or so that someone brought this to my attention. We were visiting my mother's parents' house, and at the zoo one day with a bunch of cousins, a stranger told me, 'Your brother will be like this boy,' pointing to his son who had Down syndrome. It was a rather callous way of telling a small kid, but I did not notice anything different about Puneet. I did ask my mom after reaching home from the zoo, 'Is there anything wrong with Puneet?' That's how that man made it sound that there was something wrong with him. I don't remember what my mom told me, but I remember that she cried. I think I was still oblivious to what Down's syndrome meant till quite a bit later.

We had a normal atmosphere at home, and my parents made our childhood seem like anyone else's. Puneet was a late bloomer in many aspects, and that too never felt out of the ordinary. It was possibly his inability to communicate effectively when he was a child that caused disruptive behaviour, to my recollection. He would bang his head on the floor when he was frustrated and would start crying. That was quite disconcerting. Also, as a child, he was prone to getting bronchitis a lot which would cause breathing difficulties—that was very scary. I do remember my parents having to take him to the hospital once in the middle of the night. I was very scared when he had these episodes, and I can imagine now how frightened my parents would've felt. Puneet has always been healthy once he grew out of that, for which I'm grateful.

I was busy in my own world during much of Puneet's growing up. When I was a teenager, I was self-absorbed in my own things. I do remember him always being busy and going to school—Bhartiya Vidya Bhavan—then going to Muskaan later. A scary episode occurred when he was little due to his inability to communicate with strangers due to speech issues. He got on the wrong bus back from school one day and went missing. That was a harrowing day! Searching everywhere and not knowing whether he would be back. Fortunately, some kind soul recognised he couldn't communicate and was lost and took him to the police station—that was how we found him. There are good and kind people everywhere—thanks to the Almighty.

Puneet has a very loving and fun attitude to life and everything around him. He used to joke and laugh and make people laugh with his antics when he was younger. This would embarrass me sometimes as a teenager, and I would tell mom to make him stop. He loved being around girls and women and would hug and kiss everyone that he would meet. Again, embarrassing for a teenager. I guess those were the times when I wished he would stop doing these things.

His memory is phenomenal. He remembers events, everyone's names, and everyone in the extended family and friends and keeps on asking about them. I wish my memory was half as good!

My husband and daughters have been totally indulgent and caring with Puneet. It gladdens my heart so much. He gives so much love and gets it back in reciprocation. All my friends have always treated Puneet very indulgently and do so now as well. Taking their cue from our family treating Puneet indulgently, I have not seen anyone closely associated with our family treat Puneet in a disrespectful or dismissive manner. We are blessed to have such caring and understanding family and friends.

On Muskaan

I vaguely remember the inception of Muskaan: lots of meetings at AIIMS with Dr Verma and other parents. My memories are clearer about when Muskaan was set up in the basement of a house in Hauz Khas, where the masala unit was operational. That was the time when holiday greeting cards became a significant fundraising venture at Muskaan. The cards featured designs by the children at Muskaan, and one of Puneet's designs was chosen. The days and months leading up to the new year were filled with sorting the cards, bundling them into packets, and attempting to sell them to anyone interested. Everyone, from family friends to others, was drafted in to tackle this mammoth task. It was a very hectic time for all at Muskaan, trying to secure corporate accounts to purchase large quantities and convincing individuals to buy them for personal use.

Growing up, I didn't realise at the time how much my mom was juggling. She had two full-time jobs—teaching at college and establishing Muskaan as what it is today - all while raising her family and managing our home. I am awed by what she has accomplished and how she has never seemed frustrated by the immense challenges life has thrown her way. Her inner strength is phenomenal and inspires me every day. Papa has always been a rock for all of us, supportive and encouraging of every decision Mom has made for Muskaan. He has been the driving force behind getting Muskaan to where it is now, from acquiring the land to designing the building and managing logistics to have it up and running, all with the help of his friends and colleagues. Puneet and I are so very blessed to have such incredible parents, and we must have done something right in our past lives to have them in ours now.

My husband and I have encouraged our daughters to be involved with Muskaan in any way they can. When they were in school, both spent their summer holidays participating in and helping with activities and events at Muskaan. They have grown up witnessing Muskaan's growth and have become part of the Muskaan family themselves.

Cousins Speak

Here are some observations, thoughts, and feelings that Puneet's first cousins have shared. I am very thankful to all of them for sharing it. Most of the cousins are almost the same age. They had spent significant time together during family get-togethers in vacations.

Rupali

Living in different cities means we may not see each other often, but without fail, every year around Puneet's birthday and at Raksha Bandhan, I call him because I know he eagerly awaits my call. Hearing his loving voice brings me immense joy. In a world where relationships are often measured against various factors, our brother-sister relationship remains as fresh and fragrant as ever. His presence in my life has added an extra dimension, one that we all should strive for, to become better and more sensitive human beings.

Swapna

A very important part of my sensitivity towards individuals with challenges has been having Puneet in my life as the son of my Buaji! This revelation takes me back to the time when Buaji first brought Puneet to Lucknow. I knew something was different about him. But seeing Buaji crying while bathing him prompted me to learn more. LIFE teaches you so many things as they keep happening to you! One such lesson occurred when my father was diagnosed with Parkinson's. Before that, we were not aware of such conditions.

One very dear statement of Puneet when he introduces me to someone is: '*Isne mujhe palaa hai*! [She has raised me!]' Once, Buaji had to go abroad, and she left Puneet in our care in Lucknow. Puneet must have been 8–9 years old at that time. But his remembering the care given by us during that time, till date, is so heart-warming!

My journey with Puneet has taught me to be ready for all kinds of surprises from my special friends. As you get to know them more, the distinction between 'normal' and 'special' keeps fading away! Same aspirations, need for love and acceptance, and happiness. This is what life is about! We, as a family, have NEVER felt why Puneet has come into our lives. Of course, there are challenges in certain things for Puneet. But then, who is free of them?

While working with Muskaan, I have become acquainted with many families of individuals with intellectual challenges. And it pains me to see the lack of acceptance of a person's limitations.

May God give us all the courage and understanding to diffuse this thin line between 'that' and 'this' side! You will come across a lot of exclamation marks in my piece—they all represent the wonder of life!

Shalu

Puneet is a bundle of joy with a pure heart and love for all. He exudes life and greets everyone with a hug and a smile on his face. His affection is evident, especially on occasions like Rakhi and Bhai Dooj, where he warmly welcomes me with, 'Aa Gayi meri Jaan,' showcasing his endearing nature. He eagerly anticipates such visits and occasions, demonstrating his caring disposition towards others' well-being. Despite any challenges he faces, he never complains and finds blissful happiness in his own world, free from tension and worries.

Remarkably meticulous and systematic in his work and daily routine, Puneet's organisational skills are exemplary. I often encourage my sons to learn from him, particularly in how he meticulously arranges his wardrobe. I feel truly blessed to have such a wonderful brother. May God bless him with good health and happiness!

Manu

As I reflect on our shared journey, it strikes me that Puneet and I are not far apart in age. Growing up, I don't recall anyone explicitly educating me about Puneet's Down syndrome; it seemed we just grew together, and through observation, I came to understand. Buaji, Puneet's mom, was so natural in her interactions with him that for a long time, we never perceived him as different. While he may have appeared and spoken a bit differently, his social skills surpassed mine and even exceeded those of many others. People fondly remember him for his funny, unfiltered, and genuine conversations.

Puneet possesses a profoundly loving and affectionate personality. It was fascinating to witness his interactions with older family members, treating them with the familiarity of peers. His respectful yet casual mannerisms, sometimes addressing elders by their first names, reflected his unique charm. Upon our reunions in Delhi, he would burst with joy, embracing each of us and addressing us by the unique names he had assigned. His knack for assigning names based on perceived characteristics or behaviours added a whimsical touch to our gatherings.

Additionally, Puneet demonstrates a keen understanding of complex familial relationships. Even in his younger days, he grasped the intricate hierarchy within the extended family circle with surprising accuracy.

Although his interests may have evolved over time, I recall Puneet's unwavering devotion to Bollywood movies during his youth. His room was often his sanctuary, where he would immerse himself in films round the clock, collecting cutouts from movie magazines. The iconic film *Maine Pyar Kiya* held a special place in his heart, with my sister playfully dubbed as Bhagyashree, reminiscent of the popular actress from the movie. In his innocent charm, he would express his desire to marry her in a manner straight out of a Bollywood script, creating delightful moments in his fantasy world.

Observing Puneet at the dining table revealed his passion for food, particularly rotis, and his disciplined approach to mealtime. His well-balanced plate and focused eating habits were evident, although one had to intervene to curb his enthusiasm for rotis, as carb-cutting wasn't his forte.

Poonam

My dear cousin, Puneet, embodies all that is sweet and dear. A cherished member of our family, he radiates love and affection to all who have the pleasure of meeting him. I cannot recall a time when his differences were explicitly explained to me. To me, he was simply my cousin, embraced with the same warmth and acceptance as any other family member.

Although our visits to India were infrequent, they were always marked by joyous moments spent outdoors, as well as evenings filled with Indian serials and movies on the television. Puneet is a diligent worker, consistently striving to give his best effort. Whether it's meticulously dressing himself in the morning or paying meticulous attention to detail in his assignments, he approaches every task with dedication and commitment.

An artist at heart, Puneet finds solace in painting and expresses his love for Bollywood through his passion for dance.

He affectionately refers to me as Madhuri Dixit, a nickname that never fails to bring a smile to my face. Like many of us, Puneet experiences moments of frustration and can display a temper when things don't go as planned. However, he channels his emotions much like he sees actors do in the movies—expressing his feelings and working through them, often finding peace within half an hour.

Despite his occasional bouts of frustration, Puneet shares a common love for delicious food and, like many, isn't overly fond of exercise. Nevertheless, he demonstrates discipline in his habits, finding balance in indulgence and moderation.

Our visits are always cherished, filled with heartfelt conversations where Puneet never fails to inquire about every member of the family. His capacity to love knows no bounds, and he generously shares his affection with all his friends and family. In Puneet, I find a constant reminder of the beauty of unconditional love and acceptance.

3

A Universe within a Black Hole

One of the fascinating discoveries physicists have made in 20th century is the existence of black holes in the universe. A black hole's density of matter and gravitational pull is so high that even light cannot escape it. Physicists say that there might be entire universes inside every black hole. Just as a black hole contains several universes within it, which remain invisible, similarly, the human mind may have black holes that remain below the level of consciousness. My close observation and efforts to understand Puneet's (my son with Down Syndrome) mind made me realise how oblivious we remain about the universe that each one of us carries in our minds, trivialising it by terming them as 'individual differences'. As I was developing insights about disruptions within me caused by his disability and comprehending Puneet's world, it raised my consciousness about the diversity of the worlds that each person brings with oneself. I saw in my son another way of being that was hard to imagine. If Puneet had not been there in my life, it would have been quite improbable to know the universe that unfolded in my life. He lives a life where every day is a fresh day, living in time-free zone, freedom from preconceived notions and biases, and abundant capacity for unconditional love and happiness.

As I was observing him through his reactions to variety of life situations, it struck me that he is not seeing the world as I did. In fact, he showed me how an unbiased mind without unnecessary ego trappings may work. Much of our experiential world is a construction of our own minds, bringing out different and unique perceptions, feelings, and reactions to the events around us. In this long journey across births as per Indian spiritual traditions, we collect various tendencies that give us a variety of propensities in life. As a psychologist, I am unable to find a better answer than 'law of karma' (a fundamental assumption in Indian spiritual knowledge systems) for explaining the uniqueness of each individual that we see around.

All efforts to teach Puneet about the concept of time, numbers, and money did not work fully, though he devised his own ways to tune into a given time schedule that had relevance to his needs and interests. It made me realise that the so-called normal world functions on the basis of social constructs, and one starts taking it for real with little realisation that it is the interpretation that could differ from one person to another. My curiosity to understand his world came up from the fact that he had limited capacity for abstraction, which meant very small repertoire of abstract concepts that form a big bulk for majority of people. His mind was not conditioned and cluttered with conceptual categories and abstract thinking. Nevertheless, it was a 'real' world for him, just like anybody else. However, I saw that it did not affect his capacity for feelings, emotions, aspirations, and psychological and social needs. His world was much simpler uncluttered by more complex abstract concepts that are normally part of our everyday transactions with the world. It also meant that his experience of the world was not filtered by the many complex concepts that we take for granted.

I noticed that he would not feel angry if people ignored him. He still wanted to be friendly with people. He was always ready to learn, even though he met with many failures in learning. He resented not being included in sports and activities that other children of his age or older children were doing. He enjoyed life without bothering about how others were judging him.

Life was becoming more and more an enigma for me, giving immense push to existential questions that I had since my adolescence. It intensified my spiritual quest. The urge to understand the essence of life and living became overpowering. I was eager to undertake any efforts that seemed to throw some light on my questions. Vedanta provided a direction to explore my search and questions. If Vedanta gave a direction to my thinking, Puneet provided several situations to test those ideas. Moreover, it demanded that I put my insights and understanding into practice while dealing with myself and situations around me. He has been my biggest teacher in life. I learnt several valuable lessons by observing him in myriad life situations and from his presence around.

Was it easy to reach to this new consciousness? Not at all. I saw how my notions, vanity, perfectionist attitude, and intellectual arrogance were creating barriers in accepting him in my life. Puneet was not creating any special difficulties for me. Like any other baby, his growth had to be nourished, assisting him in developing many required skills to live a self-reliant life.

Difficulties were arising from the social structures, norms that we unwittingly adopt in life and start believing them to be gospels. We all hold an image of an ideal child and aspire the same for our children. We are disturbed when this image takes a beating. Moreover, we start fulfilling many of our own aspirations through our children. Their accomplishments become ours, and their failures become a source of our frustrations. I realised how our social conditionings prevent us from cherishing people and situations as they are, rather than being judgemental all the time.

In the web of this dynamics, we forget that each one of us is born to experience this wonderful world according to our own unique psychological propensities. Loving care and nourishing environment help in unfolding the unique script of life that we bring with us when we are born. Our role as parents is to provide nourishment for fuller growth of our children, not only in terms of abilities and achievements but also as good human beings. This includes imbibing universal human values that promote and sustain harmony in society.

It wasn't easy to bring this much-needed shift in my thinking. It required years of inner churning of thoughts and emotions to unfold this new consciousness. I observed in Puneet so much zest for life, interest in people and environment, and it touched my heart. I found it unfair that he should always be looked at through the lens of disability/deficiency. I gradually started realising the uniqueness of his world view that he was bringing to life. It made me realise that we all experience our world in unique ways, and we are quite alone in that. The world is, after all, a construction based on our unique mental capacities and inherent tendencies that enable us to build concepts and constructs. Does a fish, bird, or animal live in the same world as we humans do? Which world is real?

Uncommon Challenges Demand Uncommon Strengths

Life is a series of challenges, and every challenge can be met with realistic solution. The sooner we take it up as a challenge and start working towards finding solutions, the stronger we become. That is the only option we have if we aspire to live life with peace, happiness, and a sense of fulfilment.

Every crisis brings with it an opportunity to find creative solutions, an occasion to unfold new meanings and learnings. For me, having a child with intellectual disability was not only a huge crisis but also a situation to question myself. I could foresee quite vividly how my life as well as my family was going to be affected by it, and that was quite disturbing and painful. I had no choice but to face it. I never liked to live with a feeling of victimhood. I always needed to find a solution to the problems coming my way. It often entailed a thorough analysis of the situation, understanding the underlying reasons and looking for the best possible ways to deal with it. It also required breaking free from egocentric ways of thinking and looking at issues from diverse and larger perspective. It demanded objectivity in understanding the nature of the problem and its solution. It brought a shift from emotional reactions to an objective assessment of the situation and its demands.

Life before Puneet

I have always found myself imbued with a philosophical disposition, delving deeper into my inquiries about people, nature, and everything that sparked my curiosity. Possessing a strong intellectual bent of mind, I valued rationality and refused to merely conform to societal norms; I sought my own reasons for accepting or rejecting ideas. Another concern that gripped me was the prevalence of social injustice in my surroundings. It kept strengthening my existential concerns. Books were my constant companions.

I liked to associate with older people to learn life's wisdom, as I found that people of my own age group had different interests. I yearned to experience and experiment with new things in life. I knew I was cut out for teaching and research, and soon after my marriage, I set out for that even though I had a small daughter. I was blessed with a caring family, and my strong commitment to my duties gave me a certain kind of freedom that enabled me to pursue my inclinations without any guilt.

Puneet was born a month after I submitted my PhD thesis in Psychology. I eagerly anticipated the arrival of my second child and had decided to postpone taking up a teaching job to relish the growing-up phase of my child. At that time, my daughter, six years old, was a complete delight in every way. I was very happy and contented with my life. However, it was not to continue like that.

Life changed when my son was born in April '76. The doctor informed us that he had Down Syndrome and would have intellectual underdevelopment. This revelation shattered me completely. Constant grief overwhelmed me, making everything look grey and lacklustre; life seemed worthless. I lost interest in everything, and looking after him became uninspiring. Despite the challenges, I pushed myself through the daily routine with acute consciousness, knowing I needed to maintain a normal environment at home for my daughter and husband.

Luckily, I secured a teaching job in July '76, which proved to be a turning point. This opportunity greatly helped in focusing my mind and energy on a demanding role that teaching brings.

It provided much-needed diversion for my mind through engagement with study and teaching, which helped me cope with my personal grief and sadness.

Exploring a New World

Puneet's presence added another dimension to my life, prompting a revaluation of societal perceptions towards people with disabilities. Viewing life through a disability lens revealed what seemed like a grave injustice. It prompted me to ponder why certain ways of being are considered less worthy? I saw the working of underlying utilitarian attitudes deep down in us. It seemed unfair that people should be judged based on their abilities and achievements. Each one of us experiences life in our own unique way. No two individuals live similar lives, and I realised that diversity is the essence of humanity and the larger world of nature.

The more I thought of it, a sense of freedom grew in me, expanding my view on life and the world. It became clear that questioning normative ways of thinking was crucial in overcoming limited and biased judgements towards people and situations. This introspection highlighted the uncertainties of life and the need for acceptance of the fact that we can't control everything that happens, but we can choose how to respond, opting for solution-oriented and growth-promoting choices.

In the midst of this, I faced the challenges of motherhood, realising that I had to find practical solutions for the demands that a growing baby presents alongside navigating through my own grief. All norms of an 'ideal' baby needed to be questioned. The so-called notions of 'normal' growth had to be abandoned without losing focus on human growth.

I understood quite early the importance of aligning myself with Puneet's world view to nurture his physical and mental growth. Our world views are based on concepts and constructs that require complex cognitive functions. When such functions are compromised, it leads to a much simpler view centred around the present moment. This realisation led me to appreciate that every mind has the capacity to learn and create a world view conducive to optimal living. Social processes should support individuals in acquiring these skills, recognising the diverse ways in which minds can adapt and thrive.

The Guideposts along the Journey

I was fortunate to be exposed to spiritual literature and learn from great Vedanta teachers. At the heart of this exploration lie fundamental questions such as 'who am I?', 'what is this universe?', and 'What is the relationship between the self and the universe?'

Vedanta and other spiritual knowledge systems offer a comprehensive perspective on life, revealing the interconnectedness of all existence. It delves into the deepest recesses of the inner world, exploring the realms of the mind (*Manas*), intellect (*Buddhi*), ego (*Ahankar*), and latent tendencies (*Chitta*). It provides profound insights into the workings of the mind by demonstrating how our psychological tendencies and desires influence our thoughts, aspirations, feelings, and reactions.

Central to this philosophy is the concept of Dharma—universal human values encompassing morality and ethics. These principles serve as essential guides for actions, facilitating the deconditioning and purification of the mind from unhelpful conditionings and thought tendencies. Particularly fascinating is the insight into the distinction between the Witness Self (*atman*) and the empirical self (ego), with far-reaching implications for our understanding of life and the universe.

Life Lessons I Learnt from Puneet

Puneet has made me learn some valuable lessons of life that I am sharing below. They made my life simpler and beautiful:

1. Everyone lives life in their own unique way, a diversity to be valued and respected.
2. In our relentless pursuit of outdoing others, we find ourselves chasing a mirage. True competition lies within, a challenge to improve within and foster personal growth.
3. We are always trying to prove our worth to others without realising that everyone is playing the same game.
4. The fulcrum of our life should reside within; otherwise, we risk being constantly tossed by external forces.
5. Our world view, along with our joys and sorrows, largely depend on our constructs, attitudes, beliefs, and conditionings.
6. Freedom from disappointments and sorrows are in our hand, and we must examine our mind space for it.
7. Stepping out of ego-centric transactions with the world opens our eyes to the wonders of life, connecting us to people around and fostering peace and harmony.

8. The search for something higher than the apparent guides us on our journey. A broader vision of life is essential for navigating the complexities of existence.

Life Is All about Love and Wonders

Living a life in accordance with dharma (universal human values) and the pursuit of connection with a higher reality or truth gradually initiate a transformative shift from ego to higher self—a feeling of oneness in all things. This connection enables us to see unity amongst all beyond apparent differences. It evokes a sense of wonder for the smallest creations of nature—be they flowers, trees, stars, cosmos, and the innumerable forms of living beings. The need for external validation diminishes, relieving us gradually from the sense of fear and insecurity. Compassion and wonder become integral aspects of our daily existence. To whatever extent this change can be cultivated, life unfolds as free-flowing beauty, transcending the confines of ego-centric concerns.

4

Navigating Shared Challenges: Insights into Family Dynamics and Coping Strategies

The earlier chapters primarily focused on my personal journey as a mother. Like me, there are innumerable mothers and families who have their own unique experiences in dealing with the disabilities of their children and adapting to such demands. Everyone has one's own ways of dealing with them. Our reactions to such situations are influenced by many factors such as attitudes, values, past experiences, and psychological constitution, impact one's responses and reactions to such situations. However, as far as challenges and difficulties are concerned, there appears to be commonality. This chapter will help identify some of the common challenges faced by families and suggests helpful ways to deal with them.

A family undergoes a major crisis when it has a member with a disability, and even more so when it is intellectual disability. It has always been considered a tragic, threatening, and distressing event and a painful situation for most parents. Generally, it triggers a great deal of anxiety, fear, sense of loss, and grief in parents. It has been observed that parents of persons with disabilities often experience chronic stress as they have to face different challenges at various stages of development—from infancy to adulthood and old age. The nature of stress spans several aspects of family life, such as daily care demands, emotional distress, interpersonal difficulties, financial problems, and adverse social consequences. Stress experienced by the families is influenced by child-specific variables such as age, gender, and severity of disability; socio-demographic variables such as class, family income, and family coping resources and strategies like acceptance of the diagnosis and perception of stigma associated with the disability. Additional stress is also created due to marital conflicts regarding bringing up a child with special needs, extra financial burdens to obtain the necessary services, and fatigue and loss of leisure time due to caretaking responsibilities.

The Indian community has traditionally been quite accepting and inclusive of differences in its members with disabilities. Though there are hardly any studies in India, rural societies appear to be more inclusive and supportive to persons with disabilities. The philosophy of karma, laying importance on the performance of one's duties and acceptance of destiny, provides a great source of resilience in dealing with adverse situations of life. However, required services are largely missing, except for some support from kind-hearted people in the neighbourhood community and friends. People generally react differently to a person with ID; some with indifference or inhospitable attitude, others with kindness and care, whereas many others—especially children—with amusement and ridicule.

The same is not true in today's urban society. Individualistic orientation and competitive spirit make people live an exclusive life with little care and sensitivity for others.

Camaraderie is often missing. It becomes a ground for negative biases, disparagement, and exclusion. The absence of needed services perpetuates biases and prejudices and greatly limits the realisation of the growth potential of children/adults with ID. It leads to immense hardships for the family in looking after care needs of the individual with ID. The families do not get any guidance and support in understanding the impact of disability on the person. It is ironic that those who need more attention and care remain neglected and least understood by society. However, families vary in terms of coping with such challenges. In my experience, some are dealing with these challenges quite effectively, whereas many reel under the heavy demands that a family member with ID poses.

Parenting Challenges

The disability of a family member itself may alter dynamics within a family, and more so if it is a severe disability or the child has cognitive or intellectual disability. Lack of proper understanding about the condition leads to powerful stigma that greatly affects the family as well as the individual with ID. We can enumerate such factors that are largely responsible for neglect and marginalisation of persons with ID:

- Stigmatisation
- Emotional reactions
- Disruption in family and social life
- Non-understanding of child's needs
- Demands on care needs and energy
- Lack of required services for children and adults with ID and guidance to parents

Stigmatisation of a Human Condition

Persons with ID appear different in their talking and behaviour. People, in general, aren't aware how to connect with them because they do not show normalcy in their actions and expressions. It often evokes a shunning attitude and a feeling of strangeness and awkwardness; thus, most people fail to connect with them. It is a common observation to see people showing a disparaging attitude, indifference, neglect, exclusion, or ridicule. It is a painful and hurtful experience for families, as it causes social embarrassment leading to grief, sadness, and guilt.

We as human beings are deeply rooted in the notion of normalcy. We feel comfortable with our own flock and identify with people of similar backgrounds in terms of social status, economic background, education, age, gender, culture, and behaviour. Influenced by this need for normalcy, we unknowingly behave in ways that hurt others. However, society behaves in such a manner because of ignorance and non-understanding of persons with ID. The answer lies in creating awareness and understanding about such conditions. It is best done by creating mass awareness about their growth potential illustrated by successful examples.

Emotional Reactions in Families

It is tormenting for a parent to find a disability in their child. Our bonding with children is so deep that we are greatly affected by their deprivations. Having a child with ID causes a blow to self-esteem, and a sense of inadequacy often creeps in. Reactions from friends and family further enhance one's frustration and anger at the child, one's own self, and others. Moreover, comparison with normalcy fills one with immense sadness. Lack of services for proper growth of the child, demand on care needs and energy, and attending to the multiple roles in life leaves no space for self-care and relaxation. It almost becomes a prolonged crisis in life that puts heavy demand on inner as well as material resources. We need to handle our grief and sadness, and at the same time take actions that are beneficial for the child and others in the family. All parents have their own journey in life, with its unique vulnerabilities, struggles, and pains. Just as all human beings respond to crisis in different ways, so do the parents with a child with ID. Few come up with a constructive response, whereas most of the families go through immense struggles and despair.

Disruptions in Family and Social Life

Taking care of a newborn itself is a demanding role. Delayed milestones in the baby cause a lot of anxiety; moreover, the diagnosis of ID can come as a severe blow. One can see how the entire life of the child and the family could be affected, as the child is likely to require support and supervision throughout life. It becomes challenging to maintain normalcy in social life because one is faced with concerns that are quite different from others. Parents wish to hear positive things about their child from others, receive loving gestures, but it rarely happens. Life does not remain normal, and it becomes difficult to sustain the same energy and enthusiasm in everyday transactions. The emotional reactions and care demand on the parents need re-adaptations in thinking and routine handling of one's role in everyday life. It is not an easy task, and it often manifests itself in disturbed reactions to everyday situations creating conflicts and disharmony in family life. Acceptance of disability is a difficult task. Though, it is a fact that cannot be altered no matter how much one wishes. The solution lies only in dealing with inner turmoil and doing our best as parents so that we help the child in their maximum growth. Meeting other parents in the same situation provides some solace as one starts feeling that they are not alone in facing those problems.

Non-Understanding of Child's Needs

A typical infant undergoes natural stages of growth and development, achieving milestones without special efforts from the parents, progressing without conscious awareness from parents who need not worry about the process. However, for a child with ID, parents must adjust their expectations and actively engage in supporting various developmental milestones such as feeding, neck control, grasping, social interaction, turning over, sitting, standing, and walking, language, and communication. The level of disability varies from one child to another, affecting the pace of progress in various areas. Speech development is a particularly significant aspect, requiring deliberate efforts to foster language comprehension and expression, either through speech or alternative communication methods. Children with severe disabilities demand more dedicated efforts and interventions.

Besides attending to basic functions, instilling discipline becomes a crucial intervention. Children with ID often express their needs in ways that may be challenging for parents to understand. Failure to address these needs can lead to problematic behaviour as the child or adult struggles to convey their emotions and desires, leaving parents uncertain about the appropriate course of action.

Despite their disabilities, the emotional and psychological needs of children and adults with ID are no different from those without. While physical needs are commonly understood, there is often less clarity regarding emotional and psychological requirements. Like any growing individual, those with ID seek fulfilment and satisfaction for these needs. The figure below illustrates a variety of such emotional and psychological needs.

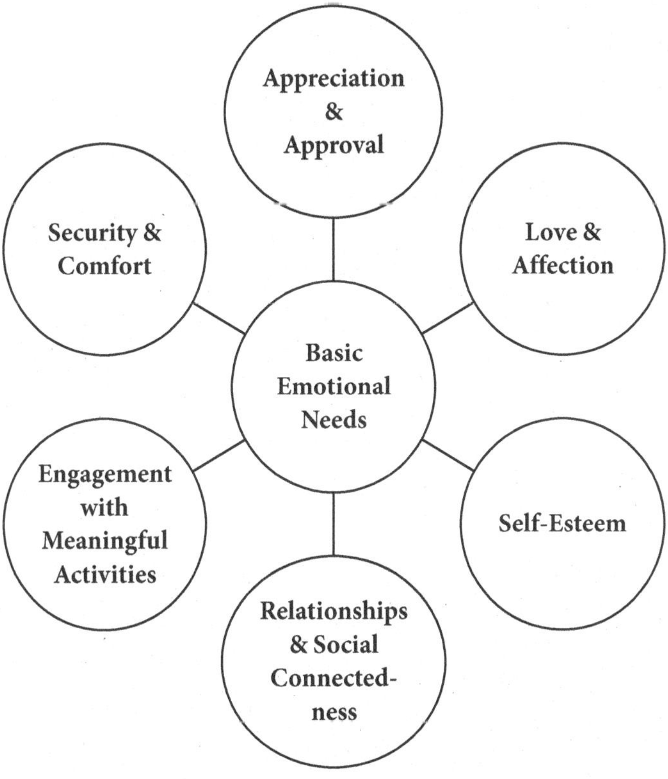

Figure 1

Non-fulfilment of these psychological and emotional needs causes disruptions in behaviour, which express themselves in the form of anger, hurt, aggression, frustration, jealousy, pain, discomfort, shame, and guilt. Fulfilling these needs is important for a healthy development of both mind and behaviour. It impacts learning capacity.

It is important to recognise that behaviour is never random; there is always a reason behind it. Moreover, it always reflects the underlying dynamics of the mind. The following figure depicts various factors that influence behaviour in myriad life situations.

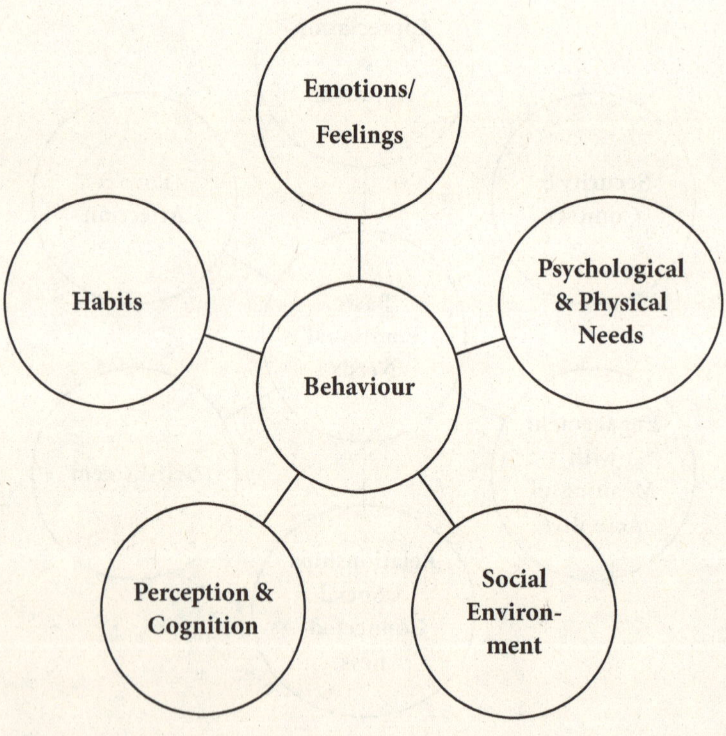

Figure 2

One needs to understand that each of the factors shown in the above figure plays a significant role in our behaviour. It is a common knowledge that our behaviour is impacted by the feelings and emotions we carry. Others' behaviour and reactions affect the way we feel in a given situation. Psychological needs, which are more subtle in their functioning, is another major factor that affects our behaviour. Similarly, our perceptions determine our behaviour. Our learnt habits reflect in our reactions, which are not easy to change.

A person with ID gets very little learning opportunity for developing necessary awareness regarding desirable or undesirable ways of expression and behaviour. Their capacity to develop perceptual and cognitive abilities is greatly underestimated by others, thus depriving them of learning several things. Explaining in simple ways, providing reasons for our expectations and other necessary information that relates to one's life builds up their ability to understand and comprehend. Experience has shown that careful training of the person will prevent many undesirable behaviours. Recognition of the emotional and other needs, positive attitude, patient handling, simple explanations of dos and don'ts, careful cultivation of helpful habits and discipline, and above all, the acceptance of the disability of the individual will facilitate healthy development in all areas of functioning. A person with ID has a great deal of intuitive understanding, so an effort in explaining things in a caring and friendly way builds their capacity for comprehension, which, in turn, acts as an agent of self/internal control, and facilitates healthy development.

Demands on Care Needs

The care demands on parents, especially mothers, are heavy. It requires immense patience and perseverance to deal with a growing child. Despite their best intentions, parents are often unable to have the required interaction and connection with the child. Teaching the child necessary skills demands long-continued efforts with patience. Being a homemaker, a mother also has several other duties to perform. The absence of adequate support and guidance to parents leaves them uncertain about making correct choices in the child's upbringing. It becomes a vicious cycle, with problems compounding, one leading to another.

It is not easy to cultivate patience and perseverance. It takes several years of work on one's thought processes, attitudes, and behaviour before one can bring about the required changes and positive transformations. Changes in attitudes and conduct cannot be easily acquired. Parents are not perfect; they, too, have their own vulnerabilities.

Challenges and Solutions in Supporting Individuals with Intellectual Disabilities

Lack of required services for children and adults with ID and guidance for parents exacerbates many struggles. These challenges could be alleviated with access to necessary services for parents and families, as well as for children with ID. A correct understanding of the disability and its impact on a child's functioning is paramount. Adopting a hopeful attitude towards the child's learning potential, coupled with realistic expectations, is crucial. This support can be provided by trained psychologists or special educators with the necessary expertise and experience.

Early education and training would facilitate the development of cognitive skills, exposure to a broader social environment, and the acquisition of various skills, including self-care and leisure activities such as sports, music, and other art forms. Adult training centres are required to provide vocational and employment-related skills. Job opportunities in supported work centres or mainstream employment can ensure a good quality of life for individuals with ID and their families.

However, such services are often scarce, necessitating their creation. More than 90 percent of such services in India and other countries have been established by parents themselves. Government support is highly inadequate, limited only to a small disability pension for the weaker economic section, tax rebates for others, and health insurance under the Niramaya scheme*. Grants for special schools or adult training centres are highly inadequate, and the process of getting the grants is tardy with delayed delivery. While government schools are expected to admit children with disabilities, the services provided are often of poor quality. Many times, these children are asked to stay at home after admission.

Parents and professionals must become the voice of their children. They need to make persistent efforts to bring the focus of both the government and society towards the needs and rights of persons with ID. This collective effort is essential for positive change, a shared experience among parents worldwide.

*The Niramaya Health Insurance Scheme in India offers affordable and comprehensive health insurance coverage specifically tailored to meet the unique needs of persons with disabilities, ensuring their access to necessary healthcare services.

Coping with the Challenges of Parenthood

Parenthood is a unique experience, giving one a sense of fulfilment, joy, and pride in one's family. It also demands great responsibility. The challenges are even more when one has a child with ID. When parents learn that their child has ID, the news comes as a tremendous blow. One feels shattered and broken. It appears as if happy days are over forever. One feels clueless regarding how to deal with oneself and with the child.

Several parents find it hard to cope with the challenges arising from attending to the care needs of their child. How a parent deals with it depends on their adaptive capacity, faith and value system, emotional resilience, inner strength, maturity, and available resources and support systems from both within the family and professionals who have prior experience in dealing with such situations. It requires a multipronged approach, as every aspect of the challenge demands a concrete solution, and it takes a long time to achieve it. Under such a condition, a parent needs to work on oneself, with the child, and the family. A multi-dimensional approach demands the care of the factors discussed below.

Acceptance and Taking Care of Oneself

Children are the centre of their parents' lives. A child with intellectual disabilities poses a serious threat to the well-being of parents. Accepting the child' condition is a huge psychological challenge in itself, and society's attitude also add to the problems. This has a negative effect on the parents' emotional health. One often comes across parents who become quite touchy and have an overriding concern about their problems compared to the problems of other people around them.

How to deal with oneself under these conditions? What efforts can be made to overcome the grief and despondency? The need of the hour is to develop an objective attitude, i.e. 'me' and 'my child' are two separate individuals with their own capacities, strengths, and weaknesses. It's important to remind oneself not to live one's hopes and aspirations through children. It is also futile to brood over things that cannot be changed. The solution lies in developing a proper attitude and careful handling. Accepting the reality as it is and developing an objective and solution-oriented approach can help us see the problem in the right perspective. No one can be held responsible for a child's condition, and nor can it be prevented. Uncertainties are part of life, and often it is not in our hands to ensure what we want. Shifting focus from one's own difficulties to the difficulties of the child helps in dealing with the situation. We, as parents, can't choose our children. Becoming a parent means being ready to shoulder the sacred responsibility of nurturing a baby into a healthy adult and a good human being. It is a test that the nature or the larger order of the universe puts us through. It is also an opportunity to learn and grow within. We need to remind ourselves of all the positives that have happened to us. If life has given us our share of problems, it has also given us our share of joys. Even a normal and healthy body is a boon. One must also remember that one is not alone; there are many parents who are in the same or even more difficult situations. Many of them are coping successfully with the challenges of rearing a child with disabilities and everything that it entails. It is important to remind ourselves that others' attitude is greatly influenced by our own attitude towards the child.

Thus, the demand of the situation is to gather strength and be aware of the responsibilities and challenges that lie ahead. A child with a disability needs much more love and care than anyone else. Parents and siblings can be a source of strength to the child. We need to remind ourselves that a person with a disability has their own struggles, needs, aspirations, joys, and difficulties. The efforts of working through difficulties are not without their own rewards. In the process, one can gain a great deal of inner strength and maturity. Dealing with one's grief and despair is important not only for oneself but for the family, too.

Below are some thoughts that may help overcome one's grief and stress:

a) It is no one's fault that a child is born with a disability. Reality has to be accepted as it is, doing what needs to be done.
b) The child's life is totally dependent on the parents; one needs to do everything possible to make life happy and meaningful for the child. It is a sacred duty of a parent.
c) Start with minimum expectations. Work for the best and prepare for the worst.
d) Love and respect the child; only then will others respect the child.
e) Share difficulties only with those who understand. Don't seek sympathy from others, as it may lead people to start pitying the child, which is a subtle form of humiliation.
f) Examine the reasons for grief, depression, anger, or frustration. One will find that these arise from distortions in one's own ways of thinking and judging.

g) Be tolerant of others' negative attitudes as they arise from their lack of knowledge and understanding. What really matters is the well-being of the child and the cultivation of one's own strength, happiness, as well as that of the family.
h) Keeping up with social life and pursuing one's interests helps in healing and normalisation of life.
i) Religious and spiritual practices can have a calming effect on our lives. Each one of us is a part of the larger order with a certain script for learning and growing. We cannot change the incidents in our life, but we can surely modify our response to them.

Nurturing Growth and Development

A major area of concern is to work towards the child's maximum possible development. Like other children, people with ID also need to learn the skills to make them self-reliant. These include a variety of manual, social, and cognitive skills. Fortunately, good reading material is available, and one can approach knowledgeable people like special educators, psychologists, and doctors, as well as speech therapists and physiotherapists who can help remove any doubts and share authentic information on the subject. Practical tips can also be found on the internet. Moreover, talking to other parents who have older children can help in several ways.

It is vital to recognise that emotional care is equally important along with other learning needs. Love, affection, encouragement, playful activities with the child, and value and respect for them go a long way in giving a feeling of psychological security and building self-esteem. This can happen when we understand the simplicity of the world of a person with intellectual disabilities. Intellectual impairment greatly reduces conceptual thinking and consequently creates significant differences in the understanding of the world. Such an appreciation will make us sensitive to the imposition of unrealistic expectations.

Psychological research has clearly shown that emotional well-being facilitates human development. The key to emotional well-being is the love and care the child receives from the parents and others in the family. Everyone needs to be loved, recognised, appreciated, and needs achievements and accomplishments to one's credit. Not being able to do some tasks is indeed quite frustrating. Creating learning opportunities is crucial as it provides experiences and builds self-confidence. It facilitates the initiative for learning new things. It is important to carefully align our expectations and learning objectives with child's readiness to acquire those skills. Parents also need to focus on the inculcation of helpful habits and discipline wherever necessary. Prevent undesirable behaviours from taking root, as it can be challenging to eliminate them later. The key is to maintain a firm but gentle approach, balancing firmness without resorting to harshness.

Many assume that children with intellectual disabilities need special and extraordinary help. Rather, when the content of most programmes is closely examined, it is found that most of them consist of activities that parents would instinctively do with their child. Much of the learning occurs through the daily interactions and activities. We need to be aware of the goals and the skills we want the child to master, which should be relevant to their life. Optimism plays e key role in strengthening our efforts.

Maintaining a Healthy Family Environment

Creating a nurturing and supportive environment is essential for the flourishing of every individual within the family. However, the dynamics within a family may change when a family member has a disability, potentially leading to disruptions in the harmony and interpersonal relations. It is crucial to address these situations with sensitivity and understanding, keeping in mind that each member contributes to the overall well-being of the family.

By embracing certain cautionary measures, outlined below, one can actively work towards fostering a positive and inclusive environment where every family member, regardless of their abilities, feels valued and supported in their unique journey. This hands-on approach not only helps alleviate tensions but also strengthens the familial bonds, promoting a sense of unity and compassion that transcends any challenges that may arise.

a) Try to resolve any differences among family members regarding the best child-rearing practices. One parent should take the dominant role in disciplining the child, while others need to assume a supportive role. Otherwise, a child may receive contradictory messages that could adversely impact the behaviour.
b) Cherish moments of togetherness and play down your problems.
c) Seek support from other family members when required.
d) Avoid burdening your other children with your problems; it will create a gloomy environment that does not benefit anyone.

e) Other children have their own growing-up challenges; understand that and be sensitive towards it.
f) As a mother, be ready to take on extra childcare responsibilities. However, do not hesitate to seek support wherever required.
g) A happy family life brings strength, harmony, and peace to its members. Unnecessary worries and complains rob us of these. Let us count our blessings and feel a sense of gratitude for them.
h) Keep up with social engagements and normal life as much as possible.
i) If we adopt the right attitude, our child will teach us some of the most important life lessons. Their capacity for love and happiness, purity of heart, freedom from biases and egoism, enthusiasm for living, and unconditional love are touching. They can transform us in a positive direction; they touch the heart and teach lessons of humanness.

Knowledge-Building

Parents are not always equipped to understand their child, especially when the child has an intellectual disability. Parents can benefit greatly from receiving knowledge and support from professionals and experienced parents who have a child with similar challenges. It's important to note that intellectual disability impacts specific mental functions rather than all aspects. It affects functions related to comprehension, analysis, reasoning, attention, memory, learning, and conceptual thinking. It makes academic learning a challenge. These functions can be substantially enhanced by focused intervention. However, many other mental functions such as feelings, needs, interests, and temperament remain unaffected. When these aspects are properly attended to and developed in the child, it promotes growth and overall well-being. Cognitive functions can also be developed and strengthened with appropriate interventions, but parents need guidance to work on them. However, daily interactions and communication play an important role in strengthening awareness and cognition.

There is an inherent nurturing tendency in every parent that pushes them to do their best for their children. This potential can be further capitalised upon if parents are able to take care of their own needs and interests. A child with an intellectual disability poses several challenges to a parent, and compassionate understanding by other members of the family, friends, and professionals helps a parent become strong and confident in dealing with such challenges.

Dealing with Social Biases

Navigating through social and cultural biases is one of the biggest challenges for families. It impacts others' perceptions. People generally hold negative perceptions about individuals with ID, which can be frustrating for both the child and the family. One needs to realise that such prejudices cannot be easily changed. The right kind of awareness in society is important to weaken such prejudices and enhance empathy and respect. Below are mentioned some ways one can use to shield oneself from negativity:

a) Do not unnecessarily talk about your difficulties with others; it should be done only with selected people who we know are sensitive and can understand the situation.

b) Take your child out wherever feasible and ignore others' stares. Try to treat it as a natural reaction considering that any newness or difference arouses curiosity in others. Very few people have the sensitivity and etiquette not to indulge in such behaviour. Avoid expressing your anger and embarrassment in such situations and treat your child with patience, love, and respect.
c) Never criticise or get angry with your child in front of others. Share their positive qualities as that helps in minimising prejudices while gaining respect for the child.
d) Value your child. Attend to them even if you are with others. It shows that your priority is your child, which, in turn, is a way of showing respect and care for the child.
e) Become an advocate for the rights of your child whenever such an occasion arises.
f) Join a parents' group and learn from their experiences and lessons.

Examining Social and Cultural Beliefs

Many people in society may be inclined to offer advice, often out of concern for both the child and parents. However, a significant amount of time is sometimes wasted on receiving spurious remedies of different kinds without any useful results. While these may provide temporary hope and emotional relief, they do not offer a concrete solution and may adversely impact the child by creating a feeling that 'something is wrong with me' or 'I am not good enough'.

Thus, it's crucial for parents to wisely consider advice from others. Practical solutions contribute to positive outcomes by nurturing a child's development and growth, rather than aiming for a 'cure'. By being discerning and embracing realistic views, parents create an environment that fosters resilience, learning, and a healthy sense of self for their children. In this way, the journey becomes more about progress and support, leading to long-lasting positive effects on the child's well-being.

Need for Joint Action

Disability should not be taken only as a personal or family issue. Beyond a point, it is a social issue. Society's attitude and lack of services impoverish the lives of individuals with ID. Thus, creating awareness is a necessary step to deal with it. One cannot do it alone. It's important for parents and professionals who have similar concerns to come together. Experience has shown that necessary services often emerge only when parents and professionals collaborate and work together for it.

There are several important areas where services are required, for instance, family support services, appropriate schooling, vocational rehabilitation, employment, and assisted living facilities. Parents need to come together to demand such services from the government, as well as make voluntary efforts themselves to create such services. I have learnt from my experience that there are many kind-hearted people around us who are always willing to support such initiatives. Moreover, all rehabilitation programmes would remain incomplete without public awareness and cooperation. Sensitive and understanding people within the community create a healthy environment for the growth and development of all children, including persons with disabilities, provided they have the right kind of exposure to disability.

Lastly, I would like to mention that life itself is a roller-coaster ride with its own ups and downs. Difficult situations provide us an opportunity for learning and growth. Here are some simple tips that can help families in constructive adaptations:

a) Conquer grief and despondency while embracing your child's disability. Life offers everyone a chance to savour this beautiful world; it's unjust to assess people based on their abilities.
b) Familiarise yourself with pertinent literature and books to better understand and manage your child.
c) Reach out to other parents facing similar situations for valuable guidance and counselling.
d) Respond thoughtfully to others' inquiries about your child, promoting awareness and dispelling ignorance and wrong notions.
e) Include your child in social events and other activities—exposure is crucial for their proper development.
f) Avoid being excessively protective—allow your child to shoulder responsibilities within their capabilities.
g) Don't worry about clumsiness or messiness; children learn through hands-on experience.
h) Provide opportunities to your child to experience success in tasks, fostering an interest in learning new things.
i) Balance the demands on you by prioritising your own needs and interests.
j) In every problem, there lies a solution. Let's seek solutions to our challenges.

k) Nurturing a child with ID presents unique situations that offer great opportunities for learning. Through them, we cultivate tolerance, patience, and compassion. Assisting them in various tasks teaches us the value of patience and perseverance. Unconditional love and acceptance enrich our core being, which transcends other achievements in life.

II
Understanding Intellectual Disability: Insights, Applications, and Holistic Development

This section delves into an understanding of intellectual disability and its impact on personal development. Various chapters within this section draw upon established knowledge in psychology and my firsthand experiences with my son and many other young adults at Muskaan (an adult training and employment centre for individuals with ID). The insights in these chapters have not only contributed to the development of Muskaan's training programs but also has helped in addressing the diverse learning needs of adults with ID.

Witnessing the positive outcomes of applying this knowledge to Puneet's growth has been reaffirming. He has developed as a mature, responsible, caring, and emotionally stable adult.

The following section addresses parents and professionals who are engaged in supporting individuals with ID. The language used has been simplified to facilitate easy understanding by the parents. It offers insights into the minds of adults with ID and their behaviour patterns. This understanding may be useful in dealing with various situations that arise from time to time while interacting with individuals with ID.

The significance of holistic development and well-being is also emphasised in this section, stressing the importance of attending to the development of a person with ID, covering emotional, cognitive, social, and behavioural aspects of personality. It may help parents in working towards a healthy growth of their child and developing insights into their minds and behaviour.

Lastly, a chapter on intelligence and cognition highlights the challenges faced by individuals with ID in this domain. Their cognitive development often remains overlooked due to limited learning opportunities. Addressing their comprehension and self-awareness can significantly enhance their self-control and self-regulation. Understanding the principles of learning and language development is key to improving their capacity for learning and communication.

5

Navigating Intellectual Diversity

One may wonder why there is so much emphasis on understanding the world of an intellectually challenged person. Careful thinking would reveal that our world is made up of concepts and constructs, and intellectual disability would limit their acquisitions. No two people live in the same world. There exist a wide variety of psychological and personality differences, such as abilities, needs, interests, though tendencies, that work towards making different worlds for everyone. It influences the way one perceives and understands the world, as well as the way one responds to it.

As a student of psychology, I have always been interested in understanding the differences among people in terms of their thinking, feelings, and behaviour. Close observation of my son's behaviour and interaction with several young men and women with intellectual and developmental disabilities at Muskaan, further added to my fascination for understanding the vast diversities in the world views that people carry with themselves.

The limited conceptual abilities and abstract thinking in people with ID reduce the complexities of their world, making it much simpler compared to others. Our conceptual abilities lead us to form concrete (objects) and abstract (ideas) concepts in the mind, and everything that we perceive and interpret is filtered through such concepts. People with ID live in a simpler and more concrete world. It is comparatively free from biases, judgements, unnecessary comparisons, and expectations. It is a pure, loving, and interesting world view where everything revolves around the present, relatively free from past baggage and worry about the future. We, as adults, start causing difficulties for them through our unrealistic expectations and judgemental attitudes.

Observing their responses and reactions to a wide variety of situations helped me in understanding their inner world of perceptions, feeling, aspirations, and needs. When I see my son welcoming all visitors to our house with affection and cheers, I like to understand what is different between me and him that prevents me from showing the same warmth and spontaneity. His responses to many situations in life are free from suspicions and filled with enthusiasm. Uncertainties of life, perhaps, do not exist for him, and it keeps him largely free of unnecessary worries.

If some of us face a lot of behavioural and emotional problems with our children, it may often mean that we could not respond appropriately to their psychological and emotional needs. Understanding, guiding, and managing their behaviour will help us if we look at their experiences and recognise their difficulties and challenges. That would help us in assisting them to learn a variety of useful behaviours. By examining their perceived world, one can speculate about the various challenges individuals with ID might be facing in their everyday lives. These are explained below.

Challenges Faced by Individuals with ID

To understand their difficulties, we need to examine their everyday living experiences and the world view they may implicitly hold. Their behaviour may be a response to these challenges or difficulties, as shown in the table below:

Challenges	Description of the obstacles they face
Non-accepting Attitudes of Others	It causes a severe blow to their self-esteem. Unconditional acceptance and empathetic interaction are foundations of positive self-image and self-esteem.
Deprivations	Their deprivations are manifold, including social exclusion, staying away from mainstream life activities, lack of appropriate communication, the absence of appropriate fun and recreation, a lack of opportunities for education and training, and a lack of meaningful role and responsibilities.
Perceived Difference in Self and Others	They sense that they are different from others but desire all that is available to their siblings or others around them.
Failure Experiences	Learning takes much longer, leading to frequent experience of failures.
Inadequate Conceptual Understanding	Lack of concepts affect their understanding of their surroundings including people and places. Such explanations are often not offered to them.

Challenges	Description of the obstacles they face
Absence of Appropriate Education and Training	The majority remain out of schools, and those few who attend are not receiving required education that can help them to learn required skills and grow into responsible adults.
Absence of Meaningful Engagement with Work	The majority do not get any such opportunity within or outside their homes. It deprives them of experiences that provide a sense of accomplishment along with friendly relationships.
Lack of Structure in Life	Families do not receive any guidance in this; it requires building a routine activity schedule in daily life and gentle persuasion to follow it.
Sexuality	No guidance is provided for channelisation of sexuality in socially appropriate forms.

Understanding the needs, perceptions, feelings, and behaviour of individuals often requires visualising their experiences by placing ourselves in their situation. Immersing oneself in the world of children or adults with intellectual disabilities (ID) could be an enlightening exercise. Limited exposure to a variety of life experiences and inadequate cognitive functioning in people with ID simplifies their world, missing many nuances that others commonly perceive. While their memory functions excel in recalling names and incidents, their semantic memory, associated with the meaning of language and situations, remains compromised.

Thus, it is evident that inadequate conceptual learning and abstraction in individuals with ID adversely impact the comprehension of the demands of varied situations. They navigate a world not designed with their needs in mind. Similarly, this is the case for a wheelchair user, or someone who is blind or deaf, who encounter limitations due to environmental barriers. Sensitivity is required to appreciate their challenges and difficulties. Moreover, non-accepting attitudes, neglect, insults, deprivations, and lack of growth opportunities exacerbate their difficulties, manifesting in undesirable behaviour and emotions. However, these challenges could be mitigated to some extent by adopting a proper attitude and sensitivity towards their emotional and learning needs, and providing them with the required growth opportunities.

Myths about Persons with ID

Several myths mentioned below are prevalent regarding people with ID. The general misconception is that these are part of their disability; whereas the truth is that most of such behaviours are reactions to the situations which they often face in their lives.

- They always remain as children and never grow beyond it
- Self-awareness and self-esteem are lacking
- Behaviour problems seen as part of their condition
- Inability to control their impulses

- They cannot learn self-discipline and self-regulation
- They are stubborn and aggressive
- They cannot learn to take care of their daily needs, learn work-related skills, and find employment
- They do not understand when we talk about them to others

Debunking these Myths

Each of the above-mentioned notions are incorrect and arise from misconceptions that are generally held by families and society.

Growing as Adults

It is a universal fact that with age, not only does the body undergo change, but the mind also matures. Everyone knows that prominent stages of physical, cognitive, and emotional development are infancy, childhood, adolescence, adulthood, mature adulthood, and old age. These changes are equally applicable to children with ID. Therefore, age-appropriate interactions are important for facilitating development and maturity. Their comprehension, capacity for self-regulation and self-discipline, sense of responsibility, and emotional understanding keep growing with age-appropriate interactions. It is true for all levels of disability.

Self-Awareness

It is crucial for self-regulation and self-discipline. Self-awareness means basic information about the body, awareness of one's feelings, likes and dislikes, discomfort, or pain. Making choices in simple, everyday situations facilitates self-awareness. The capacity for self-direction and self-regulation increases with enhanced awareness of oneself, and it enriches life.

Aggression, Stubbornness, and other Behaviour Problems

All forms of behaviour are simply an expression of our perceptions, needs and emotions. Negative behaviours mean something is troubling the person. According to Psychology, behaviour is never random and always has some underlying reason. An effort to understanding the reasons would allow us to have much better control over behaviour. Thus, we need to analyse the reasons for negative behaviour and find out its triggers. A combination of age-appropriate rewards, dos and don'ts, caring and friendly dialogue is effective in improving behaviour. It works very well in modifying behaviours if we explain why a certain behaviour is not good and actually harmful to one's self-interest. Caring and friendly communication of appreciation or displeasure is more effective in bringing desirable results rather than material rewards or physical punishment.

Learning Desired Skills and Behaviours

Persons with ID can very well learn numerous skills and behaviours needed to become more self-reliant in everyday life as well as skills that can make them employable. Employment may be in mainstream or supported employment centres where they can make a variety of products that require simple vocational skills. Training in life skills is essential to adapt to various life situations and their demands, and that should remain the focus both at home and in training institutes. Meaningful roles and responsibilities at home and work situations and engagement with productive work are time-tested ways to develop a sense of accomplishment and well-being. I have seen many examples where adults with ID are able to live a fuller life when they get such opportunities.

It is often observed that parents and other adults are unmindful of saying negative things about their children with ID in their presence. This should never be done as it is insulting to the individual. It negatively impacts their self-esteem, which is critical for healthy growth. Thus, we can influence behaviour by ensuring right perception and addressing emotional needs. The inculcation of desirable habits plays an important role in the development of healthy behaviour.

Dynamics of Human Behaviour

Perception or cognition, emotions, and behaviour have a two-way interaction with each other, as shown in the illustration below. Each influences the other and, in turn, is influenced by it. It means that we need to educate individuals with ID to develop the right understanding, recognition, and awareness of their feelings and teach the appropriateness of behaviour in a given situation. It works the same way with every person. A conscious effort to understand such dynamics will facilitate the healthy growth of mind and body. One needs to support the development of perception regarding the physical and social environment and people, cultivate awareness about the feelings of self and others, and explain why certain behaviours are good or undesirable.

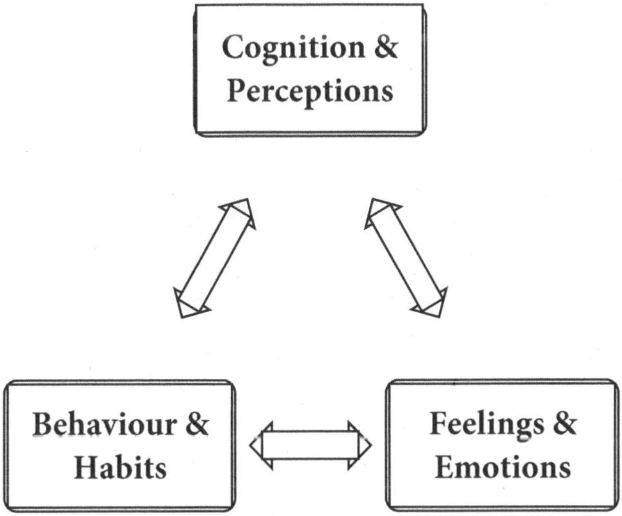

Figure 3

Barriers to Development and Fuller Life

People often underestimate the learning capacity of persons with ID, resulting in limited learning opportunities for them. They often experience neglect and marginalisation in social situations, including their own families. Since they have limitations in articulating their thoughts and feelings, others fail to understand them. They do not receive appropriate education and training inputs for the development of various faculties and have limited opportunities for the fulfilment of their social and emotional needs. The absence of growth opportunities hinders their ability to live a full life. It reflects a subtle form of injustice and an inhuman utilitarian mindset. Is it fair to dismiss them because they do not align with our societal expectations?

In the vast expanse of existence, each of us is here for a brief sojourn and has the right to live as fully as possible. People with ID are no exception. While their intellectual functions may be less developed, it doesn't diminish their enthusiasm for life or their desire to experience it to the fullest. Their unique perspective contributes to a more humane society. They provide an interesting variation to the commonly perceived world. It challenges the misguided utilitarian beliefs that devalue them because they need support to live a safe and dignified life.

6

Maximising Learning Potential: Principles and Strategies

The human mind is designed for learning, giving us a unique ability to be flexible and adapt to the demands of varied situations of life. We not only adapt but also change situations to suit our survival needs and many other human needs. We learn new behaviours that help us in better adaptations. This significantly improves our chances of bodily and psychological survival. Compromised brain development in individuals with ID may adversely affect the extent of learning potential as well as capacity for adaptation. However, despite their disability, they can still learn a variety of simple skills and concepts that help in responding to everyday demands, though their learning capacity decreases with their severity of ID.

Psychology offers several theories that explain how we learn. Two such main explanations are—learning by association and learning by insight. Learning by association means that we learn to associate two experiences that happen close to each other in space or time. It happens when two things are linked, and we form a connection between them. For example, we can learn the meaning of the word 'hot' by associating it with hot tea or milk. Similarly, we can learn the meaning of 'cold' by associating it with ice.

Learning by insight involves forming new connections amongst objects that appear different but share some common features, for example, learning the concepts of fruits, vegetables, and clothing, etc. Despite apparent differences, a commonness of certain features is recognised by the mind, and such experiences are grouped under a given category like 'fruit', etc. A conscious application of these principles will help in teaching many simple concepts.

The process of learning starts soon after birth. It is a mental process where the brain plays a major role. Whatever may be the reason for ID in an individual, it always points towards deficiencies in the development of brain and nervous system. It leads to a compromise in the learning ability and other cognitive functions in a person. However, research in this field has revealed certain factors that facilitate learning in an individual with ID:

1. They learn better through concrete examples, i.e., they learn by doing. For instance, teaching them about numbers is easier if they learn how to count objects used in daily life. Teaching desirable and undesirable actions is easier if explained through specific examples instead of simply explaining the idea of good and bad in an abstract manner.
2. A task needs to be broken into simple steps from simplest to most complex one. Starting with simple steps and moving on to complex steps will give them the experience of success and gradually enable them to learn more complex skills. It is applicable to all kinds of skill learning, such as wearing clothes, washing hands with soap, bathing, including many other higher skills.

3. Constant practise is vital in facilitation of learning. There may be an initial resistance, but a gentle nudge, concrete rewards, or appreciation are effective.
4. Try to make learning fun as it stimulates both interest and motivation. Motivation helps learning. Observe the individual to find out what works best for them.
5. Visual and other aids using touch and hearing play an important role in facilitating learning.
6. Provide immediate feedback to improve the learning of a task.
7. Keep instructions short and clear to avoid confusion.
8. Transfer of learning can be challenging for individuals with ID. This involves using what has been learnt in one context and applying it to different situations. For instance, understanding the idea of dirty and clean clothes is one thing, but generalising that knowledge to the floor, room, utensils, or a mirror can be difficult.
9. Showing keen interest in the student while helping them is important. Genuine expressions of satisfaction and appreciation by parents and teachers is the best kind of reward.
10. Keep in mind that every effort at helping the student to become independent is valuable. It helps them in taking charge of their life as much as possible. It reduces their dependence and enhances sense of competence, self-esteem, and dignity.

Learning Life Skills

There are two major areas of learning that can empower individuals with ID to live a wholesome life. These are life skills and vocational skills. Life skills refer to abilities that facilitate effective functioning across various aspects of life and foster adaptability in diverse situations. Examples of such essential life skills include self-care, social and emotional competencies, learning self-discipline, cognitive skills, awareness of self and others, understanding the physical and social environment, engagement with work and leisure, establishing a daily life structure, managing sexuality, maintaining nutrition and health, and coping with the challenges of old age and parental loss. Unfortunately, the necessity for life skills training is often overlooked by parents and educators. Life skills play an important role in the holistic development of an individual. These skills enhance adaptability both within the home environment and in external situations.

The table below illustrates significant life skills and their importance in enhancing overall efficiency for a more complete and meaningful life.

Learning	Defining	Benefits
Self-Care	Taking care of oneself by eating and drinking properly, washing hands, attending to toilet needs, bathing, maintaining oral hygiene, dressing up, grooming, and recognising health problems.	Increases self-reliance, reduces dependency on others, builds self-esteem, and lessons the workload on parents

Learning	Defining	Benefits
Self-Discipline	Following a routine in daily activities, to dos and don'ts of behaviour according to the situation, maintaining discipline in eating and hygiene, and exhibiting good interpersonal interaction.	Cultivates self-regulation, reducing the need for constant care, develops, self-respect and confidence, increases sociability, provides dignity to life
Social and Emotional Competen-cies	Understanding emotions in oneself and others, navigating social situations for appropriate behaviour in various settings (e.g. home, school, with friends/relatives, restaurants, social events, and marketplaces	Enhances social acceptance, increases social inclusion, fulfils the need for social connectedness, enhances image in the community, increases adaptability
Cognitive Skills	Sustaining attention, improving observation and memory, learning concepts, reasoning, simple problem-solving, and planning according to one's ability	Enhances mental functioning, improves learning potential, enables independent functioning in various situations

Learning	Defining	Benefits
Awareness of the Self and Others	Recognising one's needs, feelings, basic knowledge of one's body and its organs, understanding gender and age differences, and understanding of social situations	Increases social competencies, enhances self-direction—reducing dependency on others, fosters self-control, enhances emotional well-being—promoting a healthy mind and freedom from behavioural problems
Awareness of Physical and Social Environ-ments	Knowing the location of the house, school, workplace, friends' houses, recreational places, recognising weather conditions, knowledge of potential dangers, understanding people, social events, and situations	Provides context for appropriate actions in given situations and prepares for social etiquette
Work and Leisure	Understanding the duties and roles at home or workplace, developing habits for sustained activities according to one's interests and preferences	Offers role clarity and expected performance, creative productivity in leisure activities, builds self-esteem, facilitates emotional well-being, minimises negative behaviour

Learning	Defining	Benefits
Structure in Life	Forming habits for routine activities at appropriate times (e.g., sleep, waking up, bathing, meals, exercise, and leisure activities)	Greater sense of control and discipline as well as reduced responsibility on caretakers
Managing Sexuality	Expressing sexuality appropriately, under-standing privacy, and distinguishing between public and private spaces	Reduces concerns about inappropriate behaviour for parents
Nutrition and Health	Learning about nutritious food, the harmfulness of junk food, and connecting food habits with health and sickness	Provides rationale for expected eating behaviour, improves health consciousness, enhances health compliance
Coping with Old Age and Parents' Death	Discussing ageing, diseases, health problems, readiness for medicines and doctor visits, and explaining death and its universality, emphasising the importance of self-reliance to cope with parents' death	Imparts knowledge about the absence of parents after death provides emotional preparedness for facing such situations

Learning	Defining	Benefits
Language and Communication	Comprehending spoken language, increasing the use of language for self-expression, and utilising non-verbal means of communication	Enhances interaction with people, provides relief from fears and anxieties through expression, and facilitates emotional catharsis

Vocational Training and Employment

Vocational and other employment-related skills are equally crucial. Adulthood, being the longest span of one's life, consists of meaningful roles and responsibilities. We often fail to recognise its importance in the lives of people with ID, which is largely responsible for their impoverished life. Drawing from my thirty years of experience at Muskaan, focusing on the training and employment of adults with ID, I have observed that it not only provides meaningful engagement of their time and energy, but it acts as therapy. Engagement with structured programmes and activities reduces their behavioural problems and emotional difficulties while enhancing their ability to adapt to various life situations. It provides them a defined role, opportunity to develop friendships, and increased respect within their family and communities.

There are various simple vocational skills that individuals with ID can easily learn. Tasks that are structured, involve simple hand operations, and do not require complex judgement can be learnt effectively by them. Many such vocational activities, such as making paper products, food items, bakery goods, squashes, pickles, and craft items, have been successfully undertaken by individuals with ID.

Muskaan has developed three employment models catering to adults with a wide spectrum of abilities, ranging from mild to severe conditions:

1. *Supported Employment*
   A group of young adults work in assembly line method under the supervision of a supervisor.
2. *Mainstream Employment*
   Individuals working in mainstream settings perform identified roles with periodical guidance from a job coach.
3. *Employment for Adults with High Support Needs*
   Adults with high support needs work on simple products in a small teacher-taught ratio.

These three models can accommodate the needs of almost 80 per cent of the population with ID. They entail substantial training in skill learning, work ethics, and other related requirements. These supported employment models accommodate the needs of adults with varying levels of abilities, as well as creating opportunities for the fulfilment of many other needs such as sports, recreation, fun activities, creative art, craft, and festivities.

Summarising the above discussion, one can say that training in life skills and employment-related skills improves the quality of life of individuals with ID through better adaptations and defined roles and responsibilities. It gives them a sense of accomplishment, opportunities for social interactions, and helps them become useful and contributing members of society.

Language and Communication

The role of communication and language cannot be underestimated. It is central to our lives as it is empowering and provides avenues for self-expression and interpersonal interaction. Through communication, we receive and share information, access our thoughts and emotions, and develop awareness about ourselves, others, and the surrounding environment. Both verbal and non-verbal communication are important in interpersonal communication. Facial expressions and hand gestures convey significant information about a person's feelings and mental state.

Communication involves exchange of information using spoken language or other non-verbal means, such as sign language used by deaf individuals. Non-verbal expression is integral to verbal communication, even small babies respond differently to smiling and frowning faces. Children with ID often start using gestures or unclear sounds to indicate their needs and desires. This is a crucial stage where one needs to encourage and facilitate the use of words and clarity in speech without discouraging the use of gestures or sounds. Language development takes time, often several years. It may start with incoherent sounds, slowly leading to articulation of words and simple sentences. Initially, it may be unclear and slowly acquire clarity of speech comes slowly with much-needed intervention. Consistent practise, stimulation, and encouragement are essential to facilitate the development of receptive and expressive language. It is the key in facilitating the comprehension of spoken language in an individual with ID as well as speech development.

Intellectual disability is always associated with limitations in communication and language. Higher the disability, greater is the limitation in speech and language development. Its potential often remains untapped because of inadequate training inputs as well as the tendency to underestimate their capacity. Appropriate intervention in developing language and communication skills has proven to be beneficial to all, regardless of the degree of disability.

One often encounters comments from parents and others that their child with ID understands much better than they can speak. This reflects an important aspect of language development. Comprehension of speech typically begins earlier than the ability to speak. In other words, receptive language tends to develop before expressive language. Language inputs, in terms of spoken words, lay the foundation for expressive language. This underscores the significance of engaging in conversation with the child without underestimating their language potential. Associating words with objects and experiences helps the child in acquiring meaning.

Similarly, practising the pronunciation of words in playful ways helps in the development of speech and clarity in pronunciation. One may observe that children or adults with ID may often show deficiencies in the clarity of speech. They may say something that seems irrelevant and out of context. On such occasions, a parent or teacher needs to offer gentle reminders and make the person aware of the context and relevance of the content being spoken. It is helpful to provide alternative expressions for what one wants to say in such situations. These conversations should be encouraged as they fulfil one's need for social interaction. Gentle correction tends to be more effective rather than criticism, especially in the presence of others.

Language development continues throughout life if one receives proper opportunities for the same. Our vocabularies expand, and we keep learning new concepts. Just like others, people with ID keep growing in their learning of language by adding more complex expressions and learning new vocabulary. They require active inputs for enhancing communication and language ability, which is often missing in most cases. Persons with ID are known to be deficient in incidental learning, i.e., self-learning by observation. Therefore, deliberate efforts in training and other interventions become important.

Several organs play a role in language development, as outlined in the following table. Speech organs, ears, brain, and human interaction work in coordination with each other to facilitate language comprehension and expression.

Factors Influencing Language and Communication	
Speech organs	Respiratory system—windpipe, chest muscles Phonatory system—tongue, lips, teeth, palate, pharynx, alveola, and glottis
Brain	Language areas in brain, specifically the left brain
Hearing	Sensory mechanisms of outer, middle, and inner ear, as well as the auditory nerve
Conceptual learning and social interaction	Concepts are conveyed through words with specific meanings. Social interactions offer opportunities to gain exposure to information about people, situations, and the environment

The brain has specific areas devoted to language and communication, and these develop with the maturity of the brain, especially in the first 3–5 years of age. A child learns to receive and comprehend spoken language much earlier than they can speak, and this process begins in the early months of life. Human interaction plays a major role in the acquisition of language and communication. Similarly, hearing enables a child to distinguish a variety of sounds, imitate them, and combine them into meaningful words and sentences. It is illustrative to note that children who are deaf or blind also develop language through touch. However, technology has helped deaf-blind people to use vocal language as well.

As explained in the chapter 'Nurturing Cognitive Growth in Individuals with ID', people with ID have deficiencies in cognitive and adaptive functions. It affects the extent to which one can understand more complex thoughts and situations. These deficiencies vary from person to person, as they are affected by the levels of ability and learning experiences. One of the cognitive functions that is important for language and communication is conceptual learning. Concept learning is at the root of language and communication. Concepts refer to a class of objects and experiences with several common features. The concept of 'chair', for instance, may include various materials (e.g., plastic, metal, or wood) or a variety of shapes. Despite these apparent differences, there are some essential features common to all chairs. Thus, it involves the perception of similarities and differences. A child with ID requires facilitation in recognising similarities and differences, and this is mainly done by associating words with the objects, like chair is different from table. Learning and memory play an essential role in acquiring all kinds of concepts.

Communication is important in the overall development of an individual. Appropriate interventions do enhance language acquisition and speech in persons with ID. Social interaction and communication affects language and overall development. Language is a tool for learning many things in one's daily life. It plays a significant role in social inclusion and interpersonal interactions. Many behavioural challenges and emotional difficulties arise because of a lack of communication or disturbed interaction with others. Efforts at facilitating the development of communication and language will certainly contribute to the fuller growth of individuals with ID.

Simple Ways to Enhance Speech and Language

Below are several techniques that can aid a child or adult with an ID in developing language and communication. It is good to incorporate these techniques into everyday interactions rather than treating them as separate activities. Consistent intervention in a playful manner can yield the desired effect.

1. Ensure normal hearing: Check if the child has normal hearing by observing their response to sounds. If the child turns towards the source of sound, it indicates normal hearing.
2. Talk to the child: Engage in conversation with the child, even if you think they may not fully understand. Much of speech development occurs through hearing and imitation.
3. Associate words with objects: Encourage comprehension by associating words with objects. Name various items in the surroundings and familiarise the child through naming and touching.

4. Balance gestures and speech: If the child uses gestures to communicate, balance understanding their gestures with encouraging them to speak. Create a supportive environment for both forms of expression.
5. Provide auditory experience: Offer toys that make sounds and play the radio or TV during the child's activities to maximise auditory and language experience.
6. Imitate sounds: Stimulate sound imitation by helping the child mimic animal sounds, train noises, airplane sounds, etc. Make it a fun and engaging activity.
7. Talk during activities: Maintain continuous talking during routine activities like bathing, dressing, feeding, or playing, maintain a continuous dialogue with the child. Name various objects and activities to enrich their language exposure.
8. Use action and words: Associate objects with actions or functions. For instance, say 'climb the stairs,' 'eat your food,' or 'draw with the pencil' while engaging in activities.
9. Explore magazines and story books: Show magazines and children's storybooks with clear pictures, naming the objects and people in the pictures. This serves as both play and training.
10. Emphasise nouns and verbs: Reinforce speech experiences by emphasising the use of nouns and verbs. Children typically learn nouns and verbs before other language components like pronouns, adjectives, and prepositions.
11. Be patient and appreciative: Understand that speech development takes time. Comprehension usually precedes verbalisation. Patience is key, and any

progress—no matter how small—should be appreciated and encouraged.

I would like to share my personal experience of using the above-mentioned techniques to stimulate my son's language development. I began conversing with him when he was barely a year old, engaging in conversations during activities such as bathing, feeding, playing, and other daily situations. His first word, 'biscuit', emerged when he was four years old, as he led me to a small cupboard where biscuits were stored. Gradually, he progressed to using two-word sentences and eventually formed complete, short sentences by the age of nine. Although his speech was quite unclear, I persisted until I comprehended his intended message. Through continued efforts and patient insistence on clear pronunciation, his speech clarity improved over time. His vocabulary has expanded, and he frequently employs complex expressions, a development that may be attributed in part to watching serials on television and our everyday conversations on topics that interest them.

Puneet talks to me about the shows he watches on TV. We keep playing jokes with each other and have fun-filled conversations. We resolve all issues through friendly dialogue and reasoned explanations, fostering a warm atmosphere of affection and care.

7

Mental Health and Emotional Well-Being

Mental health is a state of mental well-being characterised by a positive self-image, healthy emotions, capacity to adapt of demands arising in various situations, initiative for learning, and performing one's roles with responsibility. It enables people to cope with the stresses of life, realise their abilities, learn and work effectively, and maintain healthy relationships with others. It is necessarily accompanied by a sense of emotional well-being, which manifests itself in the dominant experience of positive emotions such as happiness, love, care, and satisfaction.

Emotions are important functions of our mind and personality. They not only protect us from dangers and enhance survival but also energise our behaviour, filling us with vigour and enthusiasm in our daily life. Emotions are powerful forces that influence our perceptions, thoughts, cognitions, and learnings, both in positive and negative ways. Emotional well-being is important for efficiency in actions and thoughts. It is a common experience that our efficiency goes up with optimism and confidence and gets adversely affected when we are anxious or disturbed.

Individuals with ID are no different from others in terms of their emotionality. They experience the same range of feelings, both pleasant and unpleasant, as any other person. Often, it is assumed that persons with ID are not capable to feel and understand as others do. People generally underestimate their capacity for awareness of a range of feelings within themselves as well as others, failing to attribute their behaviour problems to their experienced emotions. A general complaint from families is that their children with ID are stubborn, impulsive, aggressive, destructive, occasionally violent, and unwilling to follow the dos and don'ts taught to them. However, I have also met many parents who do not face such difficulties with their children. It means that the expression of negative behaviour should not be taken as inevitable. It always arises from some feelings that the person carries. We need to explore the reasons for negative behaviour and understand the triggers of negative feelings and emotions.

People also fail to realise the difficulties that a challenged person faces every day. Often, they are in circumstances that are emotionally and psychologically damaging, and anyone in that situation would feel angry, frustrated, and helpless. Stubborn, disruptive, and aggressive behaviour is a manifestation of their frustrations, anger, and hurt. It may also reflect a need for self-assertion. We, as parents, get so overwhelmed by the difficulties we face that we forget to notice our child's difficulties. Their problems are much more as they cannot even talk about them, nor do they know how to deal with them. Lack of training inputs and limited capacity for self-awareness and introspection limits their understanding and articulation of their feelings. Appropriate education and training inputs in this regard can greatly help control impulsive behaviour and channelise it into desirable forms of expression.

Behaviour is never random; there is always a reason behind it. It is an expression of the way a situation is perceived and felt. So, to handle and address such behaviour, we need to explore the causes that underly negative behaviours. A simple diagram below explains various factors that influence our behaviour.

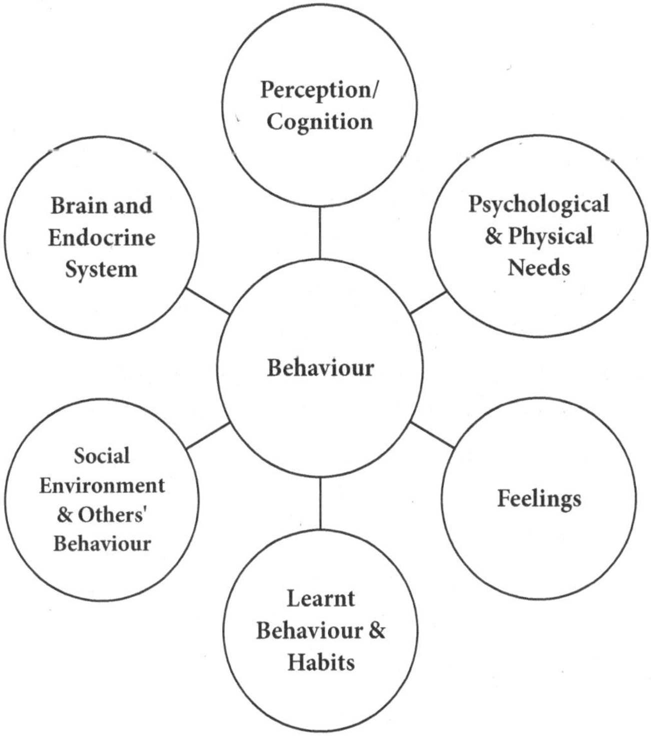

Figure 4

As illustrated in the above diagram, our actions are continually influenced by our perceptions, needs, emotions, learnt behaviour, habits, as well as the social environment, particularly others' reactions and attitudes towards us. The intricate interplay of the brain and hormones also influences our behaviour in subtle ways. We will briefly examine each of these factors below.

Perception/Cognition

How we perceive others is not solely determined by what they say or do but also by how we perceive them. We tend to project our own thoughts, feelings, and needs onto our interpretations of people and situations. Balancing the two requires objectivity, which is particularly difficult for persons with ID. They are governed by their needs and emotions. They receive little guidance in understanding situations and people. Lack of proper knowledge and awareness can make them more susceptible to impulsive reactions. To avoid such reactions, they need simple and clear explanations of the issues and situations that are relevant and important to them. For example, some individuals are afraid of climbing up and down the staircase, and they refuse to take stairs. The behaviour arises due to fear of depth. Our efforts should aim at reducing fear through proper and simple explanations and support until one gains confidence in undertaking such an activity. It may take months of counselling before fear reduction takes place and the individual is comfortable taking the staircase.

Needs and Desires

These are universal human attributes that exert subtle influences on our behaviour and personal development. While we are mostly aware of physical needs such as hunger, thirst, and avoidance of pain, the same is not true of psychological needs, which are outlined in the table below. These are powerful forces in determining our behaviour.

Psychological Needs

Need for love and nurturance	We all experience a sense of well-being when we receive love and care from others, and similarly, when we can reciprocate those feelings.
Need for approval, appreciation, and recognition	Feeling appreciated and having our thoughts and actions positively reinforced also contributes to our overall satisfaction.
Need for achievement and sense of competence	There is a need to continuously learn and achieve competence in any given task, as it provides us with a sense of confidence, and self-worth.
Need for control and power	Controlling our own lives and, to varying degrees, influencing others and life situations, is crucial for our sense of empowerment.
Need for affiliation and connectedness	Building connections with others, such as family, friends, and neighbours, is something we naturally desire.
Need for self-esteem and accomplishments	Recognition and respect from others contribute to our positive self-perception, fostering a sense of confidence.
Need for autonomy and freedom	Having the freedom to exercise our preferences and make choices within certain boundaries is essential for our well-being.

Most of the time, we have a vague recognition of our psychological needs. It requires a great deal of introspective analysis of experiences before one gains some clarity about their influence on thoughts and behaviour. Insight into oneself is a very complex mental function, which is difficult for persons with ID. It places demands on parents or other caregivers to observe, understand, and be sensitive to such needs.

Emotions and Feelings

Just as our psychological and physical needs influence our behaviour, similarly, our emotions and feelings also greatly impact behaviour. Both emotions and feeling are terms that refer to how we feel in different situations, ranging from pleasant to unpleasant. Human beings can experience a wide range of emotions, some of which are positive and some negative, as summarised in the table below:

Positive Emotions	Negative Emotions
Love and affection	Anger
Happiness and joy	Aggression
Calm and peace	Hurt and insult
Feeling of comfort and security	Jealousy
Self-worth	Frustration
Satisfaction and comfort	Pain and discomfort
Self-respect and difnity	Shame and guilt

We all have a fairly good idea about the reasons for positive and negative emotions mentioned above. The general rule is that positive experiences, such as love, acceptance, care, respect, and appreciation, create positive feelings, whereas their absence or non-fulfilment can make us unhappy. Enhancing positive experiences and feelings will lead to emotional security and well-being. It will reduce undesirable behaviour and encourage initiative for learning and a sense of responsibility.

Habits and Learnt Behaviour Patterns

Individuals with intellectual disability function better within a structured environment and are more comfortable with routine. The inculcation of good habits is a part of creating a structured environment. Helping them acquire good habits in terms of hygiene, personal care, responsibility towards oneself and others, and social etiquette is beneficial not only for them and their families but also enhances their respect and social acceptability. Although training should commence early and be consistent, it is never too late to learn. I have seen in several cases where parents could not balance between autonomy and control with regard to their children, resulting in a refusal to obey needed instructions. Neither too much autonomy nor too much control is beneficial.

Parents often underestimate the need for discipline when their children are young. It is essential to recognise that the child will grow into an adult, and parents will age. Instilling good habits and a sense of responsibility helps in the development of well-adjusted and mature adults.

These psychological factors work universally, regardless of ability level, education, social and economic status, or temperamental disposition. Addressing such needs not only enhances their well-being but also contributes to the mental well-being of parents. Love and kindness are universally recognised for benefitting both the giver and the recipient.

Social Environment and Others' Behaviour

The social environment is shaped by people through their expectations and behaviour. Positive social environment includes acceptance and respect, mutual warmth and care, responsibility within families and social groups. Conversely, being critical, angry, finding faults, and lacking warmth in relationships create an unhelpful social environment.

Brain and Hormones

While it is well-known that the brain and hormones influence our emotions and behaviour, it is less known that our behaviour and feelings also impact them. In recent years, one finds a great deal of emphasis on mental and physical health, stress-free living, and various relaxation techniques to calm the mind. Our attitudes and perceptions play an important role in calming our mind and promoting health. This interaction between body and mind is equally true in the case of individuals with intellectual disabilities. Training for enhancing their cognitive skills facilitates them in understanding what is beneficial.

Managing Behavioural and Emotional Problems

Individuals with intellectual disabilities benefit from positive interpersonal interactions. It enhances their positive experiences and feelings. Friendly dialogue and positive interaction need to be done to enhance their mental health and sense of well-being. As we have seen in the above discussion, behavioural problems have some underlying reasons. One needs imagination and empathy to understand the causes of such behaviours. It is an expression of their unhappiness and difficulties felt by them. Others may be unknowingly creating some difficulties and frustrating their core psychological needs. One needs to carefully observe their everyday lived experiences by putting oneself in their position. Their problematic behaviour may be a reaction to challenges and difficulties that are faced by them. Such challenges are elaborately explained in the chapter 'Navigating Intellectual Diversity.'

Sexuality is another aspect of development that often causes high levels of anxiety and concern in the parents. They do not know how to address these needs. It is important to recognise that ignoring or wishing away these needs is not a solution. The sooner we acknowledge and understand these issues, the better equipped we will be to guide our children or adults towards appropriate expressions of sexuality within societal norms. Inappropriate expressions need to be discouraged, and they need to learn to maintain privacy for some actions. One has to help them in channelising their sexuality through creative self-expression e.g. sports, hobbies, friendships and other avenues of entertainment.

Individuals with ID face various psycho-social challenges in their daily lives, often lacking the necessary support to overcome them. Their emotions such as hurt, anger, and frustration may manifest in undesirable behaviours. They need understanding and support in overcoming their difficulties.

Challenges Faced by Parents

Bringing up a child with ID and supporting them through various stages of life is not easy. It is important to acknowledge these challenges so that they can be dealt with effectively, making life easier for all family members. The absence of proper guidance and support services makes it difficult for parents to navigate through these difficulties. Reactions from other family members, relatives, neighbours, and friends further compound these problems. Some of these challenges are briefly mentioned in the table below.

Challenges Faced by Parents	
Blow to self-image grief, and sadness	It is difficult to deal with as it demands objectivity and shift from one's own difficulties to needs of the child.
Social embarrassment	Non-normal appearance and behaviour often invokes ridicule reactions from others.
Acceptance of disability	Unconditional respect and acceptance of the child is required.
Absence of knowledge and guidance	Parents often do not understand the nature of ID and its impact on the individual, leading to a lack of proper training for the child.

Challenges Faced by Parents	
Lack of support services	Various support services are lacking in society, or services are highly inadequate as compared to the actual needs.
Demand on time and energy	Child rearing is demanding and even more so when a child has certain impairments.
Need for developing high level of patience and perseverance	Perseverance and patience of a monk is required because the child's growth is much slower and demands interventions at each step in the everyday life.
Demand on financial resources	Medical expenses and therapy needs may be higher; moreover, one may also need external help in managing daily responsibilities.
Family discords	In many families, the mother faces unhelpful emotional reactions from other children, husband, or extended family members. Maintaining an emotional balance in such situations becomes challenging.

The above challenges are not insurmountable. Most of them demand working on one's own attitudes and emotional reactions. It requires building knowledge and understanding of the impact of ID on a person. I have deep empathy for parents dealing with enormous demands on themselves. Managing the challenges of raising a child with ID requires immense patience, perseverance, empathy, objectivity, emotional maturity, ceaseless energy, and constant balancing of various roles in life. It's a tough but not impossible task. Any positive change that we may bring in ourselves builds our inner strength and maturity. It has the potential for transformations that will positively help in many other areas of life, which isn't easy for everyone to build. Worldwide, the experience has shown that joining parents' support groups can be beneficial. Being part of such a community provides strength by connecting with others facing similar challenges, offering insights into handling various situations, and providing healing and necessary guidance. It is almost therapeutic in nature.

In this process, parents, especially mothers, often tend to neglect themselves and their personal lives. Overwhelmed by sadness and care demands, they may find it challenging to pursue their interests, career aspirations, and social life. My advice to mothers is that they should take out time for personal care and try to pursue their interests. It helps in normalising life and creating a positive and healthy home environment. This, in turn, facilitates the healthy growth of the child and reduces overall stress and difficulties. Sensitivity towards a quality life for a person with a disability can take care of many challenges that parents may have to face later. Quality of life is ensured not only by attending to physical needs but also by fulfilling psychological and emotional needs, making the person with

ID feel like a valued member of the family through assigning doable roles and responsibilities. For a quality life, they also need growth opportunities e.g. appropriate education, vocational training, work opportunities and employment, social interaction, and safe living conditions. Making one feel like a valued member of the family through assigning doable roles and responsibilities.

Managing Challenging Behaviours

The following table outlines some commonly observed negative behaviours in individuals with ID.

Challenging Behaviours	Examples of Challenging Behaviours	Emotional Needs behind Behaviour
Self-injurious behaviour	Hitting oneself, banging head	Frustration, helplessness, desperate effort to draw attention
Aggression	Throwing things, screaming	Frustration, anger
Violence	Hitting others, destroying things	Anger, frustration
Repetitive talk	Saying same things again and again	Need to communicate
Self-talking	Talking to oneself loudly	Social needs
Stubbornness	Not listening to instructions, not budging from an action	Self-assertion, expression of need for autonomy

Challenging Behaviours	Examples of Challenging Behaviours	Emotional Needs behind Behaviour
Self-centred	Serving to own needs disregard to others	Ego-centrism
Using abusive language	Use of indecent words or language	Imitating others, macho feeling
Hoarding	Irrational hoarding of useless things	Insecurity, possessiveness

Mental health problems, particularly disruptions in self-esteem, have clearly been shown to contribute to a majority of mental and behavioural problems. This manifests itself in feelings of insecurity, which in turn give rise to anxiety, fears, depression, disturbed relationships, stubbornness, and reduced efficiency in learning and other forms of adaptive behaviours. All challenging behaviours arise from underlying needs, emotions, and learnt habits, which are not unique to individuals with ID. Understanding and addressing these behaviours require a similar approach used for typically developing individuals. All children, including those with ID, can grow out of them with learning and guidance from parents and teachers. Limited insight into oneself makes it difficult to bring changes in behaviour; therefore, persons with ID need much more handholding.

The majority of behaviour problems reported by families in their challenged children stem from hyper-anxiety and inadequate self-esteem. Parents are already dealing with their own challenges in managing family and work demands, which are compounded manyfold when raising a child or adult with ID. Limited psychological and material resources further complicate the situation, creating a vicious cycle that contributes to problems rather than alleviating difficulties. The tension within the family adversely affects everyone involved.

Often, parents also have limited psychological and material resources to deal with the demands on them. Thus, a vicious cycle sets in where each one contributes to problems rather than doing something to reduce the difficulties. It escalates the tension in the family that adversely affects everyone.

For children or adults with ID, the key is to alter or remove situations that trigger undesirable behaviours. It involves repeated communication about the desirability of certain actions, emphasising how they may harm the individual. Substitute actions should be provided, and approval or disapproval should be expressed using age-appropriate methods. Pre-empting such situations can also be effective, preventing unpleasant behaviours. Daily engagement in play or other recreational activities, creative self-expression in art and craft, structured learning programmes, and friendly interactions encourages positive emotions, fostering a sense of well-being and preventing problematic behaviours.

The sense of well-being depends on feeling loved, accepted, and cared for, as well as accomplishments and independence in daily living. As children with ID grow, their behaviour patterns must change to facilitate their transition into adulthood. Psychological and emotional well-being not only addresses behaviour difficulties but also strengthens inner forces that facilitate learning and adaptability.

Challenged children provide a golden opportunity for parents to develop a humanistic orientation, empathy, compassion, patience, and perseverance. Facilitating emotional and psychological well-being not only addresses behaviour difficulties but also provides a foundation for wholesome growth.

I would like to share a personal experience with my son, Puneet, who exhibited challenging behaviours during early childhood. Through understanding the needs and emotions behind the behaviours, addressing them, and consistently communicating the undesirability of such actions, he learnt to control his behaviour. Introducing creative activities, playing sports together, and engaging in board games helped build cognitive, emotional, and behavioural patterns.

I also incorporated playful methods to teach Puneet emotions, using stories, pictures, and conversations. When he expressed sexuality at the age of 13–14, I focused on three areas—awareness of public and private spaces for expressions, teaching the social desirability of behaviour, and finding legitimate expressions aligned with his interests. Dialogues and clear guidelines, including dos and don'ts, were crucial in navigating social situations.

By the age of 25–30 years, I observed a fair amount of maturity in dealing with various social situations. This approach, emphasising dialogue and feedback, played a significant role in enhancing cognitive and emotional growth.

It is important to recognise that it is hard to bring changes once behaviour patterns are well established and have become habitual reactions. The same is true for every person. It helps if we visualise the future and determine what is good for the person and the ageing parents. Positive self-image, self-discipline, awareness of health and hygiene, helpful habits, engagement with work and responsibilities, friendly interactions, and development of interests and hobbies will go a long way in improving the quality of life and facilitating adaptations with changing life situations.

8

Nurturing Cognitive Growth in Individuals with ID

There are several troubling questions that arise in the minds of parents of children with intellectual disabilities. Why does my child lag behind other children? Why can they not think and understand like others? How is their future going to look like? Parents want to know what they can do to ensure the maximum development of their child. Unfortunately, there is not much guidance available, and many parents feel a sense of helplessness.

In this chapter, I aim to provide an understanding of the intellectual and cognitive functions of the mind that play an important role in our intelligence and understanding of the world, including that of people with ID. Children or adults with ID have difficulties in such functions and it affects their learning, as well as other forms of behaviour, collectively called adaptive behaviours. This chapter will also provide practical suggestions on the activities that can be performed in daily life to enhance and maximise the cognitive development of an individual with intellectual disabilities.

The topics that are covered in the following pages include understanding the nature of intellectual disability and its impact on a person's intellectual functions, cognition and its development, and strategies for enhancing cognitive development. Here, I have also included a few theories and models that will provide us useful ideas to understand the mind of an intellectually challenged person. I have been careful in explaining various technical terms in a simple manner to ease the understanding for parents and practitioners. These technical terms can empower parents to partner with professionals in unlocking their child's potential, facilitating optimal growth and development.

Nature of Intellectual Disability and its Impact

Intelligence can be roughly assessed through tests, and the resulting scores are known as the Intelligence Quotient (IQ). One is considered of average intelligence if they score between 90 to 110. In clinical terms, a person with an IQ of 70 score or lower is diagnosed with intellectual disability, and a score between 70–90 IQ is considered as a slow learner. IQ scores are based on a person's performance on an intelligence test that examines one's functioning on several types of activities connected with intelligence. It is only a rough assessment and should not be taken as an accurate prediction about the future functioning of a person because much depends upon the training inputs and growth opportunities that shape a person.

A great deal of research has been done in Psychology in the last 100 years on the nature of intelligence and its functioning. Like all mental functions, intelligence, too, defies detailed analysis in terms of the components that constitute intelligence. Without getting into the academic intricacies, one can say that the broad trend among psychologists is towards taking intelligence as multiple abilities rather than as a unitary capacity. It consists of the following abilities:

1. Analytical Intelligence—the ability to analyse and evaluate problems and use it to solve them.
2. Creative Intelligence—the ability to go beyond what is given and come up with novel ideas.
3. Practical Intelligence—the ability to solve problems of everyday life, adapting to the demands of the environment, and utilising the knowledge gained from experience in various life situations.
4. Emotional Intelligence—the ability to monitor one's own and others' emotions, distinguish between different emotions and label them appropriately, and use emotional information to guide thinking and behaviour.

   The four key components of emotional intelligence are: (i) self-awareness, (ii) self-management, (iii) social awareness, and (iv) relationship management.

Children with ID are often slow to reach developmental milestones, such as sitting, walking, and talking, as compared to their peers. Moreover, it varies from one child to another, depending upon the severity of the disability as well as the educational interventions received by them. They often exhibit difficulties in areas of self-care, communication, social interactions, and self-management in a wide variety of situations. Difficulties in learning are a common feature, the extent of difficulty depending on the complexity of various tasks.

Intellectual disabilities arise from suboptimal development of intellectual or cognitive functions, which limits one's comprehension and learning capacities. It has a cumulative effect on other areas of functioning as well. The following diagram shows various cognitive functions which, if optimally working, lead to average intelligence.

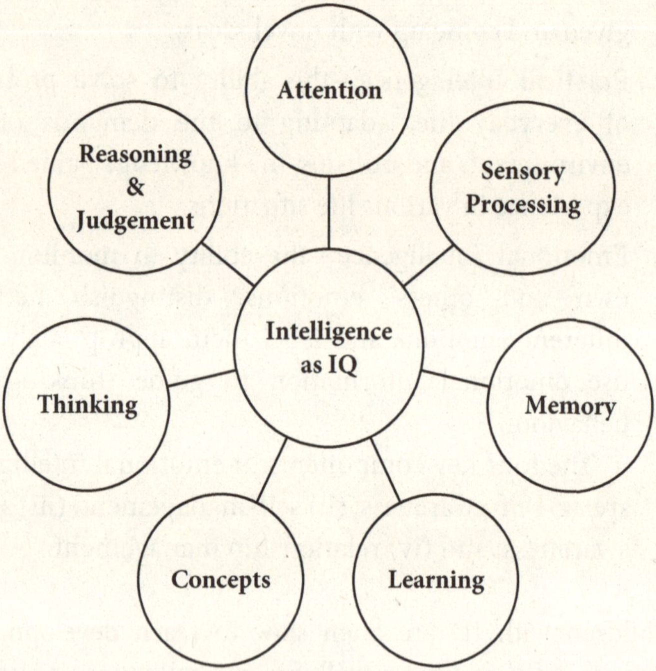

Figure 5

Cognitive functions refer to various functions of the mind that help us perceive and understand the world around us, including ourselves. A detailed discussion on the various cognitive functions that impact intelligence is outlined in the latter part of the chapter. However, it is important to note that all these functions can be significantly improved with interventions as a part of daily interaction with the individuals. It is no different from what we usually do with children, except that a conscious and focused effort helps in the development of a child with ID.

Intelligence and Cognition

While intelligence is a commonly used term, the same is not true for 'cognition'. Understanding the relationship between the two will better equip us to help a child with ID. Intelligence refers to one's abilities to learn and understand, and deal with new and difficult situations, whereas cognition refers to underlying mental processes that aid in knowing and comprehending the world around us. To a newborn baby, the world is a mix of patches of sounds, colours, smells, and touch. Slowly, as the brain matures and one is exposed to a variety of stimuli from the environment, the world starts becoming more organised and meaningful for a growing baby. Various cognitive processes play a vital role in this. Language and communication—a unique capacity of the human species—itself requires adequate functioning of cognitive processes, enhancing the scope of our learning in diverse ways.

When all these cognitive or mental functions are optimally working, it leads to average intelligence. In simple words, one may say that cognition refers to a variety of mind functions that are involved in knowing and understanding the world, whereas intelligence is the capacity arising from cognitive functions. Optimally functioning cognitive processes give us the capacity to understand the complexities of the physical and social environment and respond to its demands. Abstraction, reasoning, and flexibility in thinking help us adapt to diverse life situations. People with ID have sub-average functioning in all these areas.

Academic learning places a heavy demand on these functions; therefore, an individual with ID finds it difficult to cope with the school curriculum. Conceptual learning becomes more and more complex and abstract as we progress to higher classes in schools and colleges. Each discipline of knowledge has its own unique set of complex and abstract concepts that we need to learn before we can understand a subject, e.g., biology, mathematics, social sciences, etc., otherwise, it becomes meaningless for us. Learning such concepts becomes a challenge for people with ID. Similarly, dealing with several daily life situations also demands complex conceptual learning, such as negotiating social interactions, recognising dangers, handling financial management, responding to health-related demands, and comprehending physical environment.

It is important to recognise that though people with ID have limited cognitive capacities, but focused training and appropriate interventions can greatly strengthen and enhance these functions. It increases their capacity to comprehend and learn desired skills and behaviours that make them much more functional in everyday life. It helps them become more self-reliant and independent, reducing the care demands on the parents or caretakers. However, they may continue to require different degrees of support and supervision in many other complex areas of life.

Cognitive Functions and their Role in Learning and Comprehension

Research indicates that intellectual disability is a diverse condition, stemming from various factors, each exerting its distinct influence on brain development. The table below outlines several recognised genetic or chromosomal conditions associated with intellectual disability.

Down syndrome	It is a genetic disorder that occurs when someone is born with a full, or partial, extra copy of chromosome 21 in their DNA. One in 1000 babis may be born with this condition.
Fragile x Syndrome	Fragile X syndrome is the most common cause of an inherited intellectual disability worldwide. It is a genetic condition caused by a mutation (a change in the DNA structure) in the X chromosome. Boys are usually more affected than girls—it affects around 1 in 3,600 boys and between 1 in 4,000-6,000 girls.
Prader Willi Syndrome	It is a rare genetic disorder that affects around 1 in 10,000 to 20,000 people. This disability is quite complex and is caused by an abnormality in the genes of chromosome 15.
Brain Injury	Injury either at birth or in infancy may adversely affect brain development. Similarly, diseases like meningitis or severe jaundice in early infancy can also impact brain development.

The conditions presented in this table, along with many more undiagnosed conditions that cause ID, may exhibit their own profiles of cognitive impairments. Some functions may demonstrate less impairment than others. Therefore, each individual may manifest a unique set of impaired functions that become apparent during functional assessments. This approach provides practitioners with additional tools for intervention in training and education, thereby enhancing the overall functioning of a person.

Cognitive Functions of the Mind

The various cognitive functions listed below play an important role in learning and behaviour. Creating learning opportunities to develop and strengthen these functions will significantly improve the learning potential of every child, including individuals with intellectual disabilities.

Attention

Attention is fundamental to learning and possesses three crucial features:

1. Ability to focus attention
2. Ability to sustain attention for a minimum time period to learn or accomplish a task
3. Ability to shift attention from one task to another as per the demands of a given situation

As children mature, their attention becomes more focused and sustained. Infants may persist with an object for short durations and then lose interest, while pre-schoolers display interest in activities and objects for more extended periods. With the growth of the capacity for sustained attention, children also exhibit an increased ability to focus on task-relevant details and ignore irrelevant aspects in a given situation.

Older children, in comparison to younger ones, can flexibly adjust their attention to meet the demands of a situation. This implies that 12-year-olds can shift their attention from one aspect of a task to another more quickly and efficiently than younger children aged 5 and 6.

Several factors contribute to the development of attention, including brain maturation and appropriate training. Development of attention is facilitated by meaningful interactions, like frequent engagement with activities and conversations, age-appropriate interaction, communication with interest, task selection based on personal preferences, clear and simple conversations, and simple tasks as per the ability of a person.

Continued practise in performing various tasks gradually strengthens the ability to sustain attention, and it is a crucial aspect of any learning process. It is important to know that if a child is easily distracted, it is not a deliberate act on their part, but rather it is an indication of a difficulty in sustaining one's attention that requires support and understanding. In such cases, providing encouragement and acknowledging even small achievements can be highly beneficial.

Perception and Observation

We constantly undergo experiences involving seeing, hearing, smelling, tasting, and touching in our everyday lives, and the same holds true for newborn babies. In our brains, a series of processes collectively referred to as 'information processing' occur, resulting in organised and meaningful perception. These processes evolve with the maturation of our brains and exposure to the world. Over the past 25 years, research has identified deficiencies in three aspects of information processing in individuals with intellectual disabilities, both children and adults. In the initial stages of information processing, individuals with intellectual disabilities may not process certain fundamental aspects of sensory stimuli in the same way as those with average intelligence. For example, if you show a group of random dots in a pattern, people with average intelligence usually quickly see a shape like a square. On the other hand, those with intellectual disabilities might not see such patterns as easily. It emphasises that individuals with intellectual disabilities may not perceive things with the same level of detail as we do.

The second aspect is encoding, which involves making information meaningful. However, individuals with intellectual disabilities may take longer to encode information and may be less accurate in this process. For instance, the letters of the word 'ball' initially appear as a set of black lines on a page, but through encoding, these lines become recognised as the word 'ball'.

The third aspect involves the use of cognitive strategies. Individuals with intellectual disabilities are considered less efficient in formulating these strategies. For instance, in puzzle games with several pieces forming a given picture, individuals with intellectual disabilities may work in a random manner, requiring facilitation to organise their perception and actions. Encouraging learning through simple and clear explanations in various situations can gradually assist them in working in a more systematic way.

To strengthen perception, the following techniques can be employed:

- Creating awareness about details
- Making tasks meaningful
- Guiding attention to see inter-connections amongst given tasks

Implementing these approaches can significantly contribute to enhancing perception in individuals with intellectual disabilities.

Learning

There are two predominant ways in which we learn—learning by association, also known as conditioning, and learning by insight or understanding.

Associative learning involves the connection of two experiences that occur simultaneously or closely follow each other in time or space. For example, pairing the word 'mother' with the presence of one's mother establishes an association.

On the other hand, learning by insight entails understanding relationships among things in a new way compared to our existing knowledge. Simple explanations foster comprehension of these relations and contribute to understanding and reasoning. For instance, explaining as to why certain foods are unhealthy helps in connecting food with illness. Everyday learning situations, such as playing a game or solving puzzles, involve learning by insight.

Parents often contribute to the learning process of their children including children with ID by using both principles of learning, though they may not know its theoretical background. Engaging in repeated conversations, offering explanations on the how and why of things, pointing to objects while providing their names and explanations are effective measures for stimulating learning. It is crucial to recognise that motivation and interest play pivotal roles in our learning process. Therefore, interactions should be conducted in an enjoyable manner, accompanied by ample encouragement and rewards for the child. This may include expressing appreciation, love, and happiness for their achievements, occasionally followed by concrete rewards.

Why Academic Learning Is Difficult for Intellectually Challenged Individuals

While reading, we must engage in multiple mental skills simultaneously, such as recognising individual letters and words, translating them into speech sounds, and acquiring the ability to recognise the visual appearance of common words. Reading is an intricate process requiring a seamless coordination of various skills. The overall reading performance will decline significantly if any of these skills are underdeveloped.

Academic activity necessitates a considerable level of abstraction and language proficiency, involving intricate cognitive functions like a comprehensive grasp of complex concepts, higher memory functions, reasoning and logic, and problem-solving.

Memory

As attention improves with age, so does memory. Memory strategies such as rehearsal, organisation, and elaboration help firm up our retention of learnt tasks and behaviours. Memory development occurs with maturation as well as through learning.

Thus, repetition and providing meaning to our experiences are crucial for the retention of learnt tasks. What is often overlooked when teaching intellectually challenged individuals is that we sometimes make the repetition uninteresting, meaningless, or irrelevant to their lives, thereby failing to facilitate their learning process. In fact, parents or teachers must strive to be innovative in using learning materials and teaching methodologies when working with a person with intellectual disabilities. It may receive better cooperation of the child in learning. Research in psychology has revealed how the mind works in the process of forming our memories.

Information Processing Theory by Atkinson & Shiffrin (1968)

We receive information from the environment through the sense organs. This information goes to the first part of the system—the Sensory Register. The information is held here only for one to three seconds. Most of it disappears soon after. For example, we may remember the phone number till we write it immediately, otherwise it would soon be lost.

When one attends to or focuses on some of this information, it moves to the second level—the Short-Term Memory (STM). The STM can hold only a limited amount of information (five to nine items) for a limited time interval (10 to 20 seconds). After that, unless we attempt to rehearse and remember, this information is forgotten. The longer we can hold on to information in the STM through repetition, the greater are the chances that it will move into the third and largest storage part—Long- Term Memory (LTM). Unlike the STM, the LTM has unlimited capacity to store knowledge. This is also our permanent knowledge base. Once information enters the LTM, it is stored here for good.

> Whenever we need a piece of information, we search through the LTM to get it back. Effective recall is enhanced by using certain strategies, such as explaining and understanding, which supports the application of acquired knowledge.

Concept Formation

Concept learning is extremely important for understanding our world. Concept development helps us categorise our experiences and learn the meaning of objects, words, and experiences. For instance, tables, chairs, fruits, and vegetables are examples of various concepts. This involves categorising similar objects in one given category and associating them with a specific name. Everyone learns the concepts of varied complexity in this manner.

Concept learning and language go hand in hand, forming the foundation of our understanding of the world around us. Even if an intellectually challenged child or adult has not learnt to speak, they can still learn the meaning of words and language used in communication. However, they require persistent practise to learn such associations. Our efforts in this regard are bound to make a difference in their concept learning. It is important to recognise that concept learning is crucial for increasing one's efficiency in dealing with various demands of life because it provides meaning to experiences.

People with ID are adept at learning concrete concepts rather than abstract concepts. Concrete concepts refer to observable objects and situations, whereas abstract concepts relate to notions that cannot be easily connected to objects.

Academic learning at school becomes challenging for them because it demands a higher degree of abstraction.

Planning

Planning refers to the strategy of work, determining what should be done first, what should be done later, and how things should be done. As children grow, their capacity for planning also develops. Older children are far more systematic and orderly than younger ones and tend to plan and organise things before they begin a task.

Individuals with intellectual disabilities generally lack the ability to plan on their own. Repeated practise and experiences in planning a given task help them become disciplined and organised in their approach to routine work. It enhances their functioning and gives them a greater sense of control.

Analysis, Reasoning, and Problem Solving

These are some of the more complex cognitive functions. Simply put, it involves the five Ws: What? How? Why? Who? Where? It refers to mental or cognitive functions involved in finding reasons for certain actions, feelings, thoughts, and events. Individuals with intellectual disabilities possess elementary forms of reasoning. However, it can be enhanced by providing relevant experiences, i.e., explaining and giving reasons for why something happened. They may not be able to engage in abstract reasoning but can understand the reasoning connected to concrete situations in everyday life. For instance, why one should wash hands before eating or why should one bathe every day.

Problem-solving means applying knowledge and understanding to solve a given situation or choosing an action to deal with it. It is a complex cognitive function requiring greater degree of comprehension, application of previous learning and, seeing its relevance to the problem-solving. It requires comprehending the entire situation so that necessary actions can be taken or solutions can be worked out.

Metacognition and Self-Regulation

This term refers to awareness of oneself and one's thoughts, feelings, and needs. Metacognition helps in regulating and directing one's own behaviour. The ability for metacognition affects our performance in many ways. The capacity to regulate and discipline our behaviour without external demand and control results from the development of metacognition, and it holds true for intellectually challenged children and adults as well. However, it is critically dependent on the development of cognitive skills discussed in this section.

Metacognitive abilities naturally develop with age, but intellectually challenged individuals require deliberate support for it. They need to be made aware of themselves in terms of their emotions, likes and dislikes, discomfort, internal sensations, like hunger, thirst, pain, etc. Enhancement of self-awareness will increase the capacity for self-direction and self-control. We need to make it a consistent way of interaction with them and have trust in their capabilities of self-regulation.

How Does Cognition Develop?

Just like our body grows from infancy to adulthood, similarly, our mind and cognition also undergo a parallel evolution. Renowned Swiss developmental psychologist Jean Piaget, who created and studied an account of how children and youth gradually become able to think logically and scientifically, provides us with a broad map of this development. His specific observation focused on the significance of maturation (the process of simply growing up) in enhancing children's ability to comprehend their surroundings. Certain tasks become feasible only when they reach psychological maturity. He suggested that as children progress in age, distinct dimensions reveal themselves in their understanding of the world. According to his findings, these transitions typically occur around 18 months, 7 years, and 11 or 12 years. Illustrated below are the significant cognitive developments during a child's growth. This holds true for all children, including those with intellectual disabilities.

According to Piaget, cognitive development occurs in four stages. These stages have a fixed order and are universal, meaning they apply to all children worldwide. The stages are as follows:

1. Sensorimotor stage (0 to 2 years): During this stage, infants use their senses and motor activity to explore the world. Instead of engaging with things at a mental level, babies interact with them through their physical bodies. Mental representation, the ability to hold an image or picture of an absent object or past event, develops only at the end of this stage.

   By the end of the sensorimotor stage, infants learn to differentiate themselves from others, recognise themselves as agents of action, and begin to act intentionally, such as shaking a rattle to make noise or pulling a string to make a toy move. The child achieves object permanence, understanding that things continue to exist even when not directly sensed.

2. Pre-operational stage (2 to 7 years): During this stage, there is a significant increase in representational activity. Children become more adept at using mental representations compared to the sensorimotor stage. They learn to use language to represent objects through images and words.

   Around the age of two, children experience a leap in language development, associated with further cognitive development. Pretend play, such as games like '*ghar-ghar*' or 'doctor-doctor,' becomes essential for social and cognitive development. However, thinking at this stage is still egocentric, and children struggle to consider the viewpoints of others.

3. Concrete operational stage (7 to 11 years): This stage marks a major turning point in cognitive development. Children's thinking becomes more logical, flexible, and organised, resembling adult thinking closely. They become more capable problem-solvers but can only apply logical thinking to concrete, perceptible information.

4. Formal operational stage (11 years and older): In this stage, older children and adolescents become capable of thinking and operating on abstract information.

Piaget's theory does not view the child's mind as a simple passive receptor of information; instead, it sees the child's mind as an active processor of information. The child absorbs information from the environment and processes it according to their schemes or concepts. Piaget believed that, just as the physical body has structures, the mind also contains structures, referred to as concepts or psychological schemes. These schemes help children understand things. When a child encounters an object or information, they interpret it based on their existing psychological structures or concepts. For instance, if a child has learnt the shape of a circle, they can grasp circles of various colours and sizes. An analogy can be drawn from computers, where the hardware functions only when software programmes are installed. Similarly, the brain operates when concepts and language are acquired through learning experiences.

Considering the above discussion, what can we infer about understanding the mental operations of individuals with intellectual disabilities? Due to insufficient brain development, they often remain at the level of concrete operations with limited capacity for abstraction. Similarly, logical thinking does not develop fully. Nevertheless, there is still ample room for learning that can be capitalised through appropriate education and training. Here are a few points to keep in mind when assisting individuals with intellectual disabilities in their learning:

1. Concept learning necessitates active interaction with objects, people, and activities, combined with repeated explanations and encouragement through positive feedback. The more concepts a person learns, the better their understanding of the surrounding environment. Although language plays a crucial role, it is not a significant limiting factor. Many people with intellectual disabilities have good receptive language skills even if they are non-verbal.

2. Intellectually challenged individuals learn best through seeing, hearing, and touching, rather than abstract reasoning. Conversations should be simple and related to observable things and situations.
3. Instructions should be straightforward, avoiding overwhelming amounts of information at once. The more we simplify instructions, the better their capacity to comprehend and follow them.
4. They can develop elementary reasoning or logical thinking if parents and teachers make it a habit to explain things using the five Ws—what, why, where, when, and how.
5. People with intellectual disabilities may face limitations with abstraction, preventing them from fully reaching the stage of formal operations in Piaget's terminology. However, useful information about physical and social environment as well as self-awareness can significantly enhance their functioning in a variety of situations.
6. Motivation is fundamental to learning. Taking an interest in the individual, adopting a gentle approach, setting realistic expectations, and providing encouragement with positive feedback, even for small achievements, boosts their self-image, confidence, and initiative for learning.
7. The formation of good habits is crucial, as changing habits becomes more challenging later in life.
8. Learning is a lifelong process; it never stops.

Over four decades of hands-on experience in education, training, and employment for individuals with intellectual disabilities have unequivocally demonstrated significant improvements in their cognitive functioning. They acquire skills and competencies that boost their performance across various domains. Notably, we observe that prospective candidates seeking admission to Muskaan are now better equipped with learnt skills compared to two decades ago. This positive trend can be attributed to parents and teachers creating enriched learning environments, both at home and in school.

Intellectual disability is no longer perceived solely as limitations in an individual's abilities but also as barriers within the social environment they navigate. The social model of disability presents a revolutionary perspective, acknowledging disability as a by-product of impairment and the surrounding environment. Ample evidence supports the view that providing individuals with intellectual disabilities appropriate education, training, life skills, and work opportunities significantly improves their functioning. Embracing a supportive environment at home and at school, prioritising emotional well-being, and offering personalised support result in well-groomed, responsible individuals who become valuable assets to their families.

Above all, we must never forget that people with intellectual disabilities are, first and foremost, individuals with their own lived experiences. We should be appreciative of diverse world views they bring with them. Their world view is as authentic as others'. My close experiences of living and working with them have provided illuminating insights, emphasising that the world we inhabit is conditioned by the way our brains, minds, and cognitive functions construct it.

Enhancing Cognitive Development

Nearly all the activities in our daily lives engage cognitive functions such as attention, perception, memory, concept learning, thinking, and reasoning. These cognitive functions can be strengthened through regular daily activities, and this applies to everyone, including individuals with intellectual disabilities. There's no need for specialised activities to promote cognition. Ordinary daily activities like bathing, eating, going for outings, everyday conversations, and daily interactions provide ample opportunities to enrich a child with information.

Recognising and naming common utility items, being aware of one's needs and feelings, as well as those of others, following instructions, understanding others' expectations, knowing dos and don'ts along with the reasons behind them, and becoming familiar with the social environment—all these activities constantly tap into our cognitive capabilities. It is essential to note that conversations should be integrated into activities, making it a natural part of everyday interaction. Consistent and regular teaching is also important for achieving the desired results. The earlier we start such interactions with our child, the better would be their overall development, including cognitive functioning, would be.

Mental functions overlap with each other, meaning that working on one function will also enhance others. For example, focusing on attention will also benefit perception and memory. The same principle applies to all other areas. Every child or adult, regardless of the severity of disability, can learn self-care skills such as managing toilet needs, bathing, handwashing, cleaning the mouth, eating, and dressing. This not only reduces the caretaker's workload but also fosters a sense of achievement and self-respect, contributing significantly to emotional well-being.

Developing motor functions is important, as most physical tasks require motor skills. While it may initially seem challenging, demanding a considerable amount of time, energy, and patience, but in the long run, you will undoubtedly feel more relaxed and free from constant caregiving along with a deep sense of fulfilment.

Below are some simple activities that can be used to enhance cognitive functions.

Attention

Attention is basic to all learning. Activities given below can strengthen attention.

1. To build attention, it is important to start a task in a distraction-free environment. The idea is to sustain the individual in doing a task that evokes their interest.
2. Read simple stories with colourful pictures.
3. Engage in simple games that they enjoy, such as catching a ball, playing with blocks or toys, etc.
4. Give the child limited play material to work with, as too many things may create distraction.
5. Tasks should match the capability of the person, and they may not be very easy or difficult.
6. Engage interest by offering encouragement, appreciation, or a concrete reward.
7. Give very clear instructions on what is to be done, e.g., a colouring task should have clearly defined boundaries or dots to mark out the area to be coloured.

8. Continued practise in performing a task gradually strengthens the ability to sustain attention. This is crucial for any type of learning.
9. Even small achievements should be recognised and appreciated.

Perception or Observation

Following activities will help in developing the child's perception and organising experiences in meaningful ways:

1. Take every opportunity to talk to them and tell them about the objects of everyday life, like fan, light, food items, family members, body parts, items of daily use, etc.
2. Let the child experience the objects through all the senses—touch, seeing, hearing, taste, and smell. Whatever is relevant in a given situation. For instance, most food items have a colour, shape, size, texture, smell, and taste associated with them. When a child perceives through multi-sensory experience, the learning becomes firmer and more comprehensive.
3. Ask them to recognise the objects and people even if they do not speak.
4. Clearly and firmly state the dos and don'ts.
5. Keep your child close while you do household chores. Talk to them by naming objects and explaining their uses.
6. Playing with them, giving them various sensory experiences helps intellectually challenged individuals in making the world of experiences more organised and meaningful.

Memory

Memory is fundamental to learning and it can be strengthened through various playful activities. It is applicable to both children and adults.

1. Ask the child to point out the objects that you are asking for.
2. Encourage them to recognise familiar objects.
3. Help the child set the table, and after removing one item, ask them to recall what is missing.
4. Engage in a conversation with the child about the recent past. For example, ask them about what they had for dinner or lunch.
5. Encourage the child to share the story of their favourite book or movie.
6. Read a short story and ask the child questions based on it.
7. Ask the child to complete pictures, such as an elephant without a trunk or a face without an eye.
8. The same activities can be done with a non-verbal child by assisting them in pointing answers or using sign language or a picture board.

Concept Development

A concept is a set of rules used to define the categories of objects, things, events, people, emotions, etc. Concepts help us make sense of things and understand them. The more concepts one has, the greater their understanding and capacity for communication. Concepts can range from concrete (shape, vegetables, animals, etc) to abstract, like love, happiness, pain, beauty, quietude, etc. Concept learning is based on perception of similarity and differences in objects or experiences. It applies to all age groups.

1. Give the child sorting activities based on one feature, e.g., sort out all pens and spoons. Then progress to sorting spoons and forks, and later spoons of large and small sizes. Start with distinctively different or similar things and gradually move to subtle differences.
2. Matching involves identifying and putting together identical things. For example, give the child different-coloured pencils. Pick up a red one and ask the child to give you all the pencils that look like the one in your hand.
3. Classifying involves putting together things that share a common characteristic. This follows when matching has been understood. To develop this, sorting activities are useful. For example, in the kitchen, ask the child to put the plates on one shelf and the glasses on the other.
4. Comparing and serialising involves comparing two objects and arranging items in a graded fashion based on a specific characteristic, respectively. Comparing establishes a relation between two objects, considering aspects like size, texture, shade, etc. For example, in daily life, you may encourage comparing by asking questions like, 'Whose shirt is bigger, yours or didi's?' or 'Who is taller? Mummy or Papa?'
5. Serialisation or gradation refers to arranging in a graded fashion, either in increasing or decreasing order based on some specific characteristic. Ask the child to copy a pattern. Make a row of blocks increasing in size and ask the child to create the same.

6. Provide a row of blocks or pebbles decreasing or increasing in size and ask them to arrange them from smallest to largest and vice versa.

Learning

Learning is another cognitive function that forms the foundation of all learning and performance. Keeping in mind the following factors would help us in facilitating learning process. These are applicable to children as well as adults with ID.

1. While teaching something to a child, it is important to start with something easy. Once the child has mastered the easy tasks, gradually introduce more difficult activities.
2. Begin with what the child already knows and has learnt. This way, the child will be able to connect new concepts with those already stored in their memory. It also fosters confidence and initiative for learning. Initially, let the child work with actual objects. For counting, provide tangible objects for them to count. Later, transition to mental connections, such as counting without the presence of physical objects.
3. Set small and realistic goals for the child. Break down larger tasks into manageable steps and teach them one step at a time.
4. Allow the child to learn at their own pace. They should have the opportunity to practice and repeat skills until they are confident.
5. When teaching, it is important to narrate the entire process of an activity to the child. Discuss the materials being used and the actions being taken.

6. In the early stages, it is crucial not to vary instructions, as the child may become confused, particularly during the initial phase of learning. Use language and words that the child can comprehend; therefore, keep communication simple.
7. Sustain motivation through praise and provide regular feedback. Feedback should be immediate and given gently, even if the child makes mistakes.
8. Focus on the entire object at first, e.g., 'This is a flower.' Then, as the person begins to identify flowers, move on to details or attributes of the flower, 'It has petals and a stem.' 'It smells nice.'
9. All learning proceeds through five stages: Acquisition, learning of a new task; Fluency and proficiency, learning to perform the new task to a higher degree of accuracy; Maintenance, the skill that has been learnt must not be forgotten; Generalisation, performing the task in situations other than the one it was learnt in; Adaptation, applying previously learnt skills in a new area of application.
10. As the child learns the task, reduce physical assistance and verbal prompts. The child should be encouraged to perform the task as independently as possible.
11. As learning and performance improve, one needs to encourage the speed of working.
12. Children differ in their learning styles. Some learn better by hearing, some by seeing, and others by doing. Multisensory inputs facilitate learning.
13. Learning is a two-way process that happens through the interaction of the teacher and child. The learner must be an active participant and not a passive recipient of information, sitting and listening to a teacher.

14. The role of the teacher or parent is, most importantly, to maintain the motivation of the learner. When teaching children, it is important to make learning a fun and positive experience for the child. It is important to praise and appreciate the child's good performance and to guide them gently when they make an error. It helps a child in developing confidence and the motivation to learn more.
15. Although the processes of teaching and learning are based on some universal principles, we must remember that every child is uniquc. They have their own interests, pace of work, ability level, background experiences of success and failures, exposure, personality factors, liking for the teacher, level of self-esteem, and confidence. All these factors influence the performance on a given task. It is important for us to appreciate the child for the way they are and for what they are naturally good at.

Thinking and Reasoning

Few exercises mentioned below can facilitate thinking and reasoning:

1. Conversations with the child should include the 'what, why, how, who, and where' of events. For example, if you have brought something for your child, explain what it is, where you got it from, who gave it, why you bought it, and what the price is.
2. Explain thc reasons for the dos and don'ts that you ask your child to follow. Clarify what the results will be if these guidelines are followed or not followed.

3. Seize every opportunity to converse with your child and explain the thinking or reasoning behind it.
4. Make your explanations simple without underestimating their comprehension capacity.
5. Discuss the pros and cons of a certain action and then ask them to make a choice of action. Repeated exposure to such situations enables them to become more responsible.

Metacognition and Self-Regulation

Awareness of self is fundamental to self-direction and regulation of one's behaviour.

1. As mentioned earlier, every child, including those with ID, develops the capacity for self-awareness as they grow. However, we need to create conditions for it.
2. Encourage and facilitate self-awareness by asking about their likes or dislikes regarding food, clothes, places, and people.
3. Assist in recognising the emotions experienced in a situation, such as hurt, anger, love, etc. Extend the same inquiry to other family members.
4. Respect and value your child as they are, considering their difficulties. Trust and responsibility facilitate maturity in everyone.
5. Acknowledge and appreciate positive actions. Criticism should be delivered with care and sensitivity. Often, a more effective strategy is to ask the person themselves whether the action or behaviour was desirable or not.
6. Share your difficulties occasionally with your children, regardless of their disability. This helps

in building awareness and fostering an adult-friendly relationship.

7. Age-appropriate interactions are crucial for helping individuals with ID transition into adulthood. While they may have incomplete intellectual development, psychologically, they go through the same stages of life as anyone else.
8. Parents and teachers can foster self-regulatory skills in children and adults by creating a sense of responsibility for their actions and providing necessary feedback towards the same. Such training goes beyond just stating what is desirable or undesirable behaviour; it involves explaining why it is so. When adults tell children why and not just what to do, they provide a rationale for future action. This reinforces self-regulation and helps them learn not only how to get a particular task done but also what to do when faced with new problems.

It is important to remember that one does not need to do any special activities to build cognition. Normal, everyday activities like bathing, eating, or going out are the best opportunities to enrich a child with information. For example, bathing time can be used to talk to the child about the various objects involved in the activity. You could talk about water (what is water, what all can we do with it like drink it, bathe in it, where does it come from—the tap), you could talk about soap (what colour is it, what shape is it, how does it smell, why do we use it). You can carry on the discussion of the soap when you go to the kitchen. You can show and talk about the soap in the kitchen for washing utensils and in the manners in which it is different and similar to the soap the child used in the bathroom. Similarly, while eating you can talk to the child about which vegetable they are eating, what colour is it, which utensil they are eating it with, is it hot or cold. As a memory exercise, you may ask two or three hours later, what the child had for their last meal.

The above-mentioned tips may provide a general guide to enhance learning experiences in wide variety of situations. Continued interaction through conversation and repetition helps the child in becoming aware of important information and learn the skills. The most important thing is to provide input on a regular basis. Any teaching done inconsistently or irregularly is not likely to see desired results. Initiating these activities earlier not only makes them easier but also enhances the learning experience. Parents who engage in conversations with their children, take them on outings, familiarise them with various objects and situations, and expose them to a diverse range of experiences, along with emphasising discipline and reinforcing desirable behaviour and habits, help the child to grow into well-adjusted, disciplined, responsible, and caring adults.

Regular and consistent efforts can ensure a productive and happy life not only for the child but also for the parents. Maintaining a balance between loving and disciplining your child is also crucial. Excessive indulgence may make them overly dependent, while excessive disciplining may instil fear. A combination of both ensures that a child understands the importance of obeying rules but also feels secure in the love and protection of their parents.

Remember to appreciate every small success that your child demonstrates and convey that feeling of appreciation to them. The ultimate goal of all activities should be to develop their self-confidence and help them foster a sense of self-worth. Enjoy this journey of teaching and learning with your child. While you might encounter bumps along the way, the connection forged while navigating these obstacles will ultimately prove valuable.

III

The Long Road Ahead: Changing Hearts and Minds in Disability Discourse

This section marks a profound shift from perceiving disability as a limitation to embracing diversity. My transformative journey unfolded when I connected with individuals facing various disabilities, revealing a world often overlooked by the majority. Witnessing their determination, aspirations, and resilience exposed me to a realm that many in society remain unaware of.

As I delved deeper into the disability sector, the spirit of social injustice gained momentum, fostering the growth of a social activist within me. Muskaan became an arena for experimenting with human development and organisational management, while 'parents' movement and advocacy' documented the struggles and solutions of parents advocating for improved facilities for their children. This movement, both locally and globally, spearheaded the initiation of essential services and growth opportunities for individuals with intellectual and developmental disabilities.

Amidst all these challenges, what empowered me to triumph was an overarching life philosophy derived from Vedanta—an unparalleled system of wisdom and spiritual knowledge that explores the depths of our existence by asking, 'Who am I?' This profound perspective granted me immense peace and stability, enabling me to navigate the uncertainties of life successfully.

9

Challenging 'Normalism': Embracing Diversity in Disability

Disability is a facet of diverse human conditions that has always existed in every society. For far too long, it has lingered at the periphery of social consciousness. However, the recognition of the challenges as well as rights of people with disabilities as citizens is a recent phenomenon worldwide. Disability, in general, refers to the permanent or temporary loss or disruption of basic functions such as seeing, hearing, movement, cognition or use of other parts of the body. It may refer to several conditions where impact may or may not be visible to others. One may be born with such conditions or acquire later due to disease, injury, or old age.

The notions of disability have undergone significant changes in the past few decades, with the voices of persons with disabilities and their families playing a crucial role. There has been a major shift from the medical model to the social model of disability. The medical perspective viewed disability as a deficiency located in the person, with all deprivations in life seen as a consequence of their condition. In contrast, social models recognised the significant role of society's attitude towards disability in affecting the life conditions of people with disabilities and limiting their optimal functioning. It became evident that barriers in society, such as attitudes, lack of opportunities, and environmental obstacles greatly restricted the lives of persons with disabilities. This viewpoint is encapsulated in the preamble of the United Nations Convention on the Rights of Persons with Disabilities (UNCRPD), which states, 'Disability is an evolving concept . . . disability results from an interaction between persons with impairments and attitudinal and environmental barriers that hinder their full and effective participation in society on an equal basis with others.' As people recognised this truth, it brought about a focus on dismantling physical and social structures, creating better opportunities, and addressing attitudinal barriers that negatively impact the lives of people with disabilities. Nevertheless, it is acknowledged that the road is long and requires a change in attitudes and hearts.

Another significant shift is occurring in some quarters that is impacting the understanding of disability. It is seen as a form of human diversity, a way of being in the world. For example, a person with visual or hearing impairment forms an understanding of the world that is unique due to the absence of visual or sound images. Similarly, a person with cognitive impairments knows a world that is different in some ways because several complex abstract concepts are not part of their world. It is crucial to recognise that these are authentic experiences and world views. The tyranny of 'normalism' and the lack of support systems and opportunities greatly affect the lives of people with disabilities. Suffice it to say that everyone creates a unique view of the world, and so do people with various forms of disabilities. In the words of Allie Cannington, a young advocate and activist with locomotor difficulty, 'In order to harness the power, diversity, and innovation of our society, we must realise that our bodies and minds experience the world very differently.' It is this richness of diversity that is at the core of the diversity perspective, a powerful viewpoint that leads us towards equity and justice for all despite apparent differences.

My journey in life, my association with numerous friends and family members, including my son with Down Syndrome, made me question the notions of disability. When I read a statement like 'suffering from Down Syndrome,' I asked myself, 'Who is suffering?' The person with Down Syndrome or visual impairment is not suffering. The sighted person may see blindness as a deficiency because their world is dominated by visual images, but a person with blindness has always known the world in this way. Persons with cognitive disabilities, such as intellectual disability and autism, have their own perception of the world built on their concepts and complexity levels impacted by their limitations in cognitive capacities. This diversity needs to be recognised and understood to enable them to function by making suitable changes in the environment. It is the insensitivities of others and the lack of opportunities and support systems that create problems for the person. Whether we should call it disability or diversity is not a matter of debate to be settled by smart logic and reasoning. It is a matter of life and living. Challenging the notion of disability, prevalent for centuries, has a message that can transform the way we perceive differences in people, societies, and cultures.

Nature has incredible diversity, with each creation holding a unique place in the vast scheme of the universe. This truth extends from the tiniest living cell to the complexity of human beings. Likewise, the entire universe including plants, trees, flowers, galaxies, oceans, mountains, etc., exhibit a marvellous variety. Every form of creation is intricately connected to each other, contributing to the harmonious existence of the whole.

As Jo Chopra, writer, co-founder, and executive director at Latika Roy Foundation, writes, 'People with disabilities enrich our lives in ways we cannot begin to fathom and those of us lucky enough to be ecologists in this particular ecosystem can make grateful lists of rocks they have disintegrated and nitrogen they have created from thin air. Like the rest of us, they're here because they're here. There is no need for them to justify their existence. For just as "every cubic inch of space is a miracle", so every single species is a keystone species.'

The human species is an epitome of nature's creation. Each cell making up this body, its genetic code, organs, various functional systems, topped by the brain, reveals a fantastic work of nature. Many philosophical debates have tried to explore its essence and meaning of existence and came up with profound insights. Delving into larger questions of life is a worthwhile exercise as it expands consciousness and provides framework for deliberating on important concerns of life.

Disability is a social construct. Largely, the world of a human being is constructed out of concepts that societies develop over centuries. New knowledge keeps modifying or adding to it. We hardly realise this fact and start taking the social and other realities as if they are unchangeable. Disability is one such field that forces us to question our common-sense notions. My son and many other people with diverse forms of disability have forced me to question my notions of 'disability' and 'normalcy'. I saw various forms of injustice, discriminations, and insensitivities arising from such notions, which are largely based on utilitarian views.

People are born with certain conditions and live their entire lives with a unique set of experiences, but so does everyone else. We need to remind ourselves that the world itself, specifically the social world, is a construction built by the majority, and that becomes a norm. It does not necessarily accommodate the diverse experiences and needs of people. It is nowhere as stark as with reference to people with cognitive and psychosocial disabilities. It forces them to live at the margins of society because their world is misunderstood, and their psychological needs remain unrecognised. The larger society fails to provide the necessary psycho-social infrastructure enabling them to live as fully as possible. The lack of facilities enhances their dependence on others and reduces their functionality. Is it fair?

When I look at the world of visually and hearing-impaired people, the thought that crosses my mind is, what if the entire humanity did not have vision or hearing? The world would have been constructed differently. When I look at the world from the standpoint of people with intellectual and other cognitive impairments, I am deeply reminded of the social construction of our world. The more I think about it, the more rooted I feel about the idea that disability is contextual. As per the norms of the majority, people with a different sensory and cognitive world do become a minority, and society overlooks their perceptions, experiences, and needs. This state of affairs is disturbing. As I challenged my notions arising from social constructions, I increasingly began to appreciate the diversities of the human world and disability as a form of human diversity.

Each one of us is living in a make-believe world. Little do we realise that the perception of the world itself arises from sensory and conceptual foundations as well as experiences in a particular life circumstance. Our needs, feelings, and aspirations shape our experiential world. Similarly, knowledge, learning, and reflective thinking keep changing our world view. A deeper look at our journey of life from infancy to old age itself would show that we keep changing in the perception of our world. Thus, life is a series of social constructions. Some of them help us, whereas others create barriers. Rigid thinking, biases, and prejudices are expressions of the same. This way of looking at people and the rest of creation in nature is a liberating thought. It enables one to become more accommodative of differences and resolve conflicts and difficulties with others. It paves the way for greater harmony within and without. It certainly results in a more humane approach towards everything.

Court judgments in the last few years have highlighted the controversy surrounding ableist and utilitarian notions regarding disability. A remarkable judgment of the Supreme Court of India, disallowing the abortion of the child carried by a young woman with intellectual disability, has become a revolutionary milestone. She became pregnant as a result of sexual exploitation by a worker of a women's home. The plea was that an intellectually challenged mother would not be able to handle the duties of a mother as she herself was an orphan living in Nari Niketan. A lawyer from Chandigarh and a few NGOs contested this apprehension and took it upon themselves to support and train this young woman to take care of her child. Today, the young woman is a proud mother of a teenage daughter who is studying in school. What an immense change in the life of the woman! She has somebody of her own in life, though she herself was abandoned by her parents. This is what support systems can do for a person. Similarly, the Bombay High Court had forbidden a mother to abort her child with Down Syndrome within 24 weeks of pregnancy. The judgment said, 'Children with DS are very loving and live well,' so no reason for abortion.

With increased diagnostic methods, many foetuses must be getting aborted because they have some non-normal conditions. In such cases, the plea is that it is great suffering for the mother to bring up a child with non-normal conditions. Does somebody ask those mothers who have such children? Initially, they may have felt a sense of despair, but some of these mothers actually feel blessed in raising a child with a disability because they learnt so much in the process. The lessons they learnt in life unfolded new dimensions of experiences and inner transformations that enriched life beyond imagination.

Can life ever be free of difficulties and sufferings? In the Chinese language, the same character depicts two meanings, namely crisis and opportunity. Every crisis in life is also an opportunity for immense learnings, thereby, deepening the meaning of life. My son Puneet is constantly teaching me precious life lessons. He lives in the now, free from hankerings of the past and worries for the future. He has the capacity for pure love as he is free from unnecessary biases and expectations, which themselves form a part of social conditionings. Small things make him happy. He is free from ego trappings. He is like a friend to me; we understand each other's feelings and needs. It is very interesting for me to visualise his world, which is free from many constructs and conditionings, which has enabled me to view differences as diversities of the human world and not a threat to my egoistic perception of the world. The thought of him being 'normal' does not occur to me as I have seen the limitations of the notion of 'normalcy'.

The common-sense notion that disability is necessarily a suffering is the irony of utilitarian attitude. As an extended argument, it means we should avoid or try to get rid of all situations that may bring difficulties and grief to us. To what extent would one go on in this pursuit? Tomorrow, our healthy child, or another family member may get a terminal disease or disabling condition due to disease or injury. What will we do then? Don't tell me 'that is different!' It is the conditionings of our mind that blind us and limit our thinking. Life is a series of experiences, pleasant or unpleasant. Each experience teaches us if we are ready to absorb its lessons. Painful experiences have much greater potential to make us wiser, sensitive, and compassionate.

Challenging Selective Abortion and Utilitarian View

A new kind of eugenics is emerging in society, advocating the identification and elimination of disabling conditions in the growing foetus. An argument in favour of this viewpoint is that disability causes emotional and financial burdens on the family. However, how many of us can claim absolute self-sufficiency, never instrumental in causing pain and suffering to others?

Recent discoveries in prenatal diagnosis have intensified the utilitarian vs humanistic debate. Pragmatism suggests that any form of disability brings suffering to the person and family, justifying the avoidance of such situations as the foetus is considered a potential human being. This perspective, however, subtly insults people with disabilities. The essence of being human lies in finer human sensitivities and feelings, not crude pragmatism. Life comprises joys and sorrows, and successfully dealing with such situations enhances life, facilitating inner strengths and spiritual growth.

The notion of 'suffering' concerning disability often arises from deeply ingrained concepts of 'normalcy' and ableism. Rather than seeing individuals as 'suffering' from Down Syndrome, the real suffering stems from faulty attitudes, neglect, and the lack of needed services and opportunities. Changing such attitudes is a complex psychological process, essential for effective solutions to challenging circumstances. Pragmatism holds value in life, but not utilitarianism. The 20th century has witnessed negative consequences of this attitude, endangering the survival of life on our planet due to unchecked need and greed.

Tyranny of Normalism

A close examination of the normal vs abnormal debate raises numerous questions. It suggests that the vast majority live similar lives in terms of their day-to-day work, apparent behaviour, abilities, appearance, and need patterns, asserting that this is the best way of living, and deviation from it is less worthy or unhealthy. There is a human tendency to label those who deviate as queer and unapproachable, excluding them from our consciousness as unfortunate. Similarly, individuals with disabilities are often considered abnormal and unfortunate. Working with many of them contradicts this notion. They are not suffering from their condition, rather, they are suffering from a lack of learning opportunities, others' negative and biased attitudes, and social exclusion.

The concept of 'normal' seems to originate in the statistical concept of 'normal distribution', where the majority of people lie within mean + and -1 standard deviation. Those beyond this range are considered deviant. When applied to individuals with cognitive disabilities, such as intellectual disabilities and autism, it strips them of their personhood. Disability overwhelms the perception of others, completely ignoring that they are humans first. Many strengths that they possess, including their loving, cheerful, aspirational, and caring personalities, go unnoticed. Prejudices weigh so heavily on the mind that they are denied basic growth opportunities and care for their feelings, contributing significantly to the behavioural difficulties they often exhibit.

Implications of the Diversity Perspective

The diversity viewpoint has several implications. It allows us to see strengths in people rather than only weaknesses and to recognise the fighting human spirit that overcomes all obstacles to fulfil aspirations and desires.

The unique conditions created by physical, sensory, cognitive, and other impairments are part of the immense diversity of humankind. This opens our minds to unimaginable adaptations that the human mind is capable of. Witnessing such adaptations and capabilities inspires us to face tough situations. Acceptance and respect for diversity broaden our minds to a wider canvas of human differences at individual, community, and cultural levels. It takes us from an egocentric perspective to recognise alternative ways of experiencing and understanding the world, paving the way for mutual cooperation and support, enabling us to feel empathy and compassion for others. The boundaries between self and others start melting away. It has the potential to make life much more beautiful and build a truly humane society.

A condition becomes disabling when required facilities are not available. It is an obligation of the society to accommodate and provide facilities and services to everyone according to their needs. It is distressing to see how persons with disabilities and their families are made to feel apologetic, an attitude arising from a highly limited view. The narrow and limited views of society have resulted in a complete lack of services and infrastructure critical to people living with disabilities. For too long, the majority has ignored their needs, considering them burdensome instead of feeling guilty. What a tyranny of majoritarianism! The utilitarian attitude is so deeply rooted in the psyche of the vast majority of the population that nobody even thinks to question it. It requires some reflection on our part to recognise the inflated sense of self-importance that we carry all the time. A little reflection would reveal the ephemerality of existence. Each one of us is living our lives according to our psychological inclinations, tendencies, and circumstances. We are all part of some larger order, we live our own destinies, and one day all of us will disappear into oblivion.

Every creation in nature is sacred, and life is a precious chance to experience this amazing and beautiful world. I am inspired by the courage and perseverance of so many of my friends who have struggled much harder to achieve and fulfil their aspirations compared to others. Imagine for a moment the life of a person who uses a wheelchair. They are denied simple pleasures like going out, visiting friends, attending educational institutions, and all other public spaces. Can they go to their friend's place, restaurants, markets, and other recreational centres? Where is the accessibility, even for using the toilet? How does a person with visual impairment function in the absence of mobility and technology support? A hearing-impaired person is deprived of so much information and knowledge because the social world is dominantly based on oral communication. A person with cognitive impairment is deprived of all growth opportunities forcing them to live a neglected life. ,. Families with children with cognitive impairments have no place to go for guidance and support. It results in an impoverished learning environment as well as severe emotional difficulties. The list is endless.

Who is responsible for such deprivations? Clearly, it is we, the so-called normal people in society, who have been so self-centred that we never thought of the millions of people who also need the same public spaces as the rest of the population. Urbanisation without care and sensitivity has added countless dimensions to their problems.

Every public institution is responsible for this negligence. The benefit of technology and infrastructure rightfully belongs to every one of us. It is not a matter of favour! It is not a utopian idea. Equality of opportunity is a fundamental right of everyone. We cannot accept the insensitivity arising out of selfish attitudes in the garb that this is not an ideal world.

Interdependent Nature of Human Existence

Who is completely self-dependent? We hold the false assumption that we don't need others for our survival. Our everyday living requires many people providing essential services. It is necessary to recognise the interdependent nature of human society. Some need it more than others, due to various reasons, including age. Disability is no exception. An examination of our daily life will evidently show how dependent we are. Our lives would come to a stop if many people were not providing us with what we need, such as food, clothing, medicines, and many other essential things. We may term it as a business venture of others, but the fact is that people depend upon such systems in society. The irony is that when it comes to providing needed support systems to people with disabilities, it is seen as burdensome and an issue of charity. Needless to say, people with disabilities do have specific needs, but it can't be an excuse for indifference and negligence.

Interdependence is a key survival issue for society at large, and ignoring the needs of minorities is totally unjust. Accessible public spaces and public transportation, accessible information systems, appropriate education, employment, safe living, and family support systems are some of the important issues that need immediate attention from the government and society at large. It is important to recognise that most of the difficulties faced by persons with disabilities arise due to non-understanding of their needs, whereas most people get their needs attended to without any special provision. It is unfair that certain sections of our society remain neglected and marginalised.

Is anyone immune to disability? An accident on the road can make one lose limbs, cause paralysis, or result in brain damage. The majority of people acquire disabilities as a result of ageing and debilitating diseases. How long will we remain insensitive and unresponsive to the needs of these citizens of our country? Though technology has eased many of our day-to-day struggles, it has also given us a false sense of self-sufficiency. In pursuit of individualistic concerns, we forget the role that our families and friends play in our lives. In the early years of our life and old age, our survival hinges critically on human support. The gradual loss of family values in our society will sooner or later start impacting our lives adversely.

Inclusion and Diversity

Inclusion is a recent slogan to awaken the conscience of society towards unjust treatment of some sections of our society. It means changing the mindset and creating infrastructure and opportunities for everyone irrespective of their functional abilities. Participation in social situations is essential for living a full and enriched life. The movement towards inclusion in social spaces emerged from the perception of injustice to people with disabilities due to largescale exclusion experienced by them. The shift from disability to diversity deepens our human sensibilities. Awareness of others' needs, feelings, and thoughts bridges the gap among people, creating spirit of service and compassion. . That is true inclusion. The more we understand people who are different from us, the broader our thinking becomes, along with care and respect for differences.

The slogan of inclusion, in recent times, has taken another funny tangent. In search of talent and abilities, we have started looking for unique qualities in people with disabilities. We look for something unique or different in everyone, as if humans are worthy of our respect only when they have some qualities to boast about. Every life is precious and valuable. Every creation in the world is amazing in terms of its complexity and wonderfully functioning systems. Each neuron, cell, and tissue is a wonder. How well orchestrated is everything in the universe! But the human mind, in its arrogance, starts unfairly judging and discriminating. It arises from a false sense of pride and a deeply ingrained need for establishing self-importance.

Nature has bestowed upon us the capacity for learning, discriminative intellect (*vivek*), and wisdom. This is a unique quality of every human being. It is our responsibility to use it for supporting and not destroying nature's intelligent manifestations. We need to extend a hand of friendship and support to everyone who needs it. That alone will create a humane world where everyone, irrespective of class, caste, culture, or social background can live with respect and dignity.

10

Champions of Change: Parents Advocating for Inclusion

The 20th century witnessed two major social movements, one focused on the civil rights of all citizens, and the other on the education of girls. The latter movement opened up opportunities to explore a wide variety of interests and independence that were rather restrained for women by social systems. While men had numerous choices to lead a certain kind of life, women did not enjoy that level of freedom due to various reasons.

The conscious awakening to the civil rights of people with disabilities is a relatively recent global phenomenon. While it began in the 1940s in the West, the social consciousness for people with disabilities in India started to develop in the 1980s. Although a comprehensive history of the disability movement is not well-documented in India, several activists have written on the subject, for instance, Anita Ghai's edited book, *Disability in South Asia: Knowledge & Experience.*

Two major efforts that initiated this movement were: Organised endeavours by blind individuals to raise awareness about their struggles, and the formation of cross-disability group named DRG (Disability Rights Group) in 80s and

90s. These groups played a crucial role in the enactment of the first legislation called Persons with Disability (Equal Opportunities, Protection of Rights & Full Participation) Act 1995, passed by the parliament. The legislation brought disability issues to the forefront of society and the government. Another significant legislation, the Rights of Persons with Disability (RPD) Act of 2016 was introduced as disability groups demanded a new act incorporating major points from the United Nation Convention on the Rights of Persons with Disabilities (UNCRPD) of 2006, which India officially ratified in the same year.

The 2011 national census saw first time the enumeration of people with disabilities in India. However, it leaves much to be desired as it grossly underestimated the numbers, influenced by several social factors that distort the process of correctly collecting the required information. According to census statistics, 2.2 per cent of India's population has disability, whereas many Western countries found 13per cent to have disabilities.

The disability movement has largely been led by persons with disabilities themselves. However, in case of severe disabilities, like intellectual and developmental, it was parents who raised their voices to secure services for their children. People with intellectual and developmental disabilities form the most marginalised and neglected section of our society. They remain so even within the disability sector. Services are highly inadequate, and parents face immense hardships due to the absence of proper guidance and the lack of required services.

Unlike western countries, where institutions were created to house such children as a relief to the parents, India had a different set of demands from such families. It is important to note that in the 1940s, parents in the West began questioning the institutionalisation of their children with severe disabilities, who were sent to institutions on the advice of professionals in the field and stayed there until death. The prevailing belief was that these children needed much more care to survive, and families were unable to provide that level of care. Parents in these countries started to see the injustice in this practice and advocated for deinstitutionalisation. India had a very different approach to the issue. Parents and families in Indian society always considered that it their responsibility to support and care for children and adults with disabilities. However, the growth opportunities were missing. Parents in India began raising their voices for required services and growth opportunities in terms of schooling, vocational training, and work opportunities or employment, and safe living options in senior age, etc.

It is a common observation that social awakening for the rights of people with disabilities emerged only when they themselves raised their voices against the discriminatory attitudes of society. In the case of people with severe disabilities, parents and families became their voice, giving rise to the parents' movement. We are currently experiencing the first phase of the movement where parents are instrumental in creating various services for families and growth opportunities for individuals with developmental disabilities. These services, though highly inadequate, are largely limited to big cities, and the spread of such facilities in rural areas and small cities is almost negligible, except through community-based rehabilitation programmes run by NGOs. The second phase of the movement needs to be intensified, demanding the involvement of the state in addressing diverse needs of people with disabilities and their rights through proper policies, including implementation mechanisms and adequate fund allocation.

Achievements and Contributions of Parents' Activism

Muskaan itself was started by parents in 1982 with the help of professionals from the medical field. Similarly, many NGOs were started by parents all over the country. There are no statistics available regarding their numbers except for the registration with Parivaar-NCPO (National Confederation of Parents' Organisations), which is 245 in number. However, although the work is going on in small pockets, enough experience is now available with regard to service models addressing the need for early intervention, school education, adult training, employment and work opportunities, and safe living options. There is a need to scale up these services along with identification of best practices to develop norms and standards for such services.

Presently, there are several departments set up by the government to address the needs of persons with disabilities:

- Department for Empowerment of Persons with Disability
- National Trust for the Welfare of Persons with Autism, Cerebral Palsy, Intellectual Disability and Multiple Disabilities
- Central and State commissioners to address the grievances of persons with disabilities
- Rehabilitation Council of India (RCI), which has the responsibility of training of professionals in the field

Department for Empowerment of Persons with Disabilities was established in 2014, and the National Trust was started in 1999. However, there is not much change in services on the ground. People with disabilities are losing precious years of their lives and are largely deprived of basic necessities such as early intervention, schooling, vocational or higher education, and employment. Most of them need various kinds of support, and there is no system to provide that except through personal resources and NGOs run by parents themselves. Financial support for existing government schemes is highly inadequate and far too patchy in terms of its implementation. Whatever little work is happening on the ground is done by NGOs that sustain themselves on donations and community support. The situation is grim, and the future looks bleak because there is a lack of systematic planning to reach out to people with each of the 21 disabilities listed in the RPD Act 2016.

The setting up of the National Trust for the Welfare of Persons with Severe Disabilities worked actively for a few years, however, it has become an unresponsive entity for the past decade. It was started with great hopes but is now reduced to funding a few schemes with perennially limited funds. It is surprising that such an organisation is working without field experts guiding its plans and activities and taking care of the actual work on the ground. There is no coordination amongst various ministries who are supposed to address the needs of people with disabilities.

In the table below is a list of various schemes supported by the National Trust:

S.No.	Scheme	Purpose
1	Vikaas	Day care
2	Samarth	Respite care
3	Gharaunda	Groupe home
4	Niramaya	Health
5	Sahyogi	Caregiver training scheme
6	Gyan Prabha	Educational support
7	Prerna	Marketing assistance
8	Sambhav	Aids and assistive devices
9	Badhte Kadam	Community awareness
10	Disha	Early intervention and School Readiness Scheme for 0 to 10 years

Need for Services: Focus Areas for Government Support

As earlier stated, NGOs have gained enough practical experience in running various services over the last 40 years, and models of best practices have been evolved. The concerned government departments can benefit from the learnings of NGOs and scale up the required services. The following issues need urgent attention from the government in terms of the quality of services, as well as scaling them to reach those who are not receiving any kind of services:

1. The National Survey Organisation should carry out standalone sample survey to determine the extent of

persons with intellectual and other developmental disabilities. This survey should cover economic profiles, geographic spread, rural and urban ratio, and accessibility to state support.

2. A mass awareness programme needs to be initiated to disseminate appropriate information and build a healthy attitude. A national campaign, similar to the pulse polio campaign, should be undertaken to raise awareness among citizens.
3. Special efforts should be made to sensitise medical doctors, as they are the first contact points for parents if their child has a difficulty or disability. Disability should be incorporated into their curriculum.
4. Early intervention centres, comprising a well-equipped team, should be established. Existing NGOs with a good quality of services can take up part of this work, but they need support to sustain these services. These centres could also provide counselling, guidance, and knowledge support to parents through short-term parent training programmes.
5. Selected schools need to be equipped to address the educational needs of intellectually and developmentally challenged children.
6. An education board, a sub-committee of mainstream school education boards, needs to be constituted to formulate and guide schools in setting up curriculum, programmes and activities, and monitor the quality of education and training, with certification at the end of the training. Muskaan and other NGOs in the field can support such an initiative.

7. People with severe and profound levels of disability have the right to be provided with training and other services to facilitate their development. Support services should also be provided to their parents in the mentioned schools. Such persons and their parents are living in great stress without any societal support.
8. Work opportunities for people with intellectual and developmental disabilities should be created through various models, e.g., supported work centres, self-employment, and mainstream employment. Parents, families, and professionals should be encouraged to start work centres, supported by the government in public-private partnership. Appropriate norms for it can be developed in consultation with well-functioning NGOs in the field.
9. The salaries of all teachers, professionals, and other staff should be supported by the government. This includes salary support for professionals working at early intervention centres, schools, and work centres. Moreover, their salaries should be governed by the same norms as their counterparts in schools and other rehabilitation centres. This area has been grossly neglected so far, resulting in poor or, at best, no training. Quality of services should be the criteria for such support.
10. Group homes should be supported by the allotment of land or government flats, providing assisted living, especially when parents are very old, sick, or no longer alive. All residential projects by government or semi-government organisations must reserve a percentage of flats to be allotted to NGOs for running Assisted

Living Centres for persons with intellectual and other developmental disabilities.

11. Social security allowance should be given to all individuals with intellectual and developmental disabilities. There can be a graded system of disability allowance depending on the income of the parents or caretakers.
12. Procedures for obtaining family pension for dependent challenged wards should be simplified to ensure easy access.
13. The National Trust needs to be galvanised to respond to the needs of the sector with appropriate policies and a management structure.

Enhancing the Quality of School Education and Adult Training for People with Severe Disabilities

There is a great need to improve the quality of education and training inputs for children and adults with ID. Imparting education is not an easy process, and educating a child or an adult with ID requires much more creative understanding of the person to reach out to them. Working with such a child alone is not enough; one has to involve the whole family, particularly the mother, who is the main caregiver for a child.

To understand the psychology of a person with ID, one needs to understand the normal development processes of the mind, including cognition, emotions, behaviour patterns, and psychological needs. Unfortunately, special education courses provide inadequate knowledge to understand such complex functions of the mind. It makes them see disability rather than other aspects of personality, affecting the approach and quality of the teaching process, as well as interaction with the students. The assumption of incapacity and superficial knowledge prevents one from becoming an effective teacher. Moreover, teachers' training courses focus mostly only on children with ID and not adults, showing a lack of recognition of lifespan needs. My experience at Muskaan has shown that many behaviour and emotional difficulties arise because of a lack of recognition of their psychosocial needs.

Every adult requires responsible roles in life. Work opportunity and employment are often considered incidental, rather than a necessary condition for a good and satisfying life. Many training centres function more like day care centres and do not focus on training and education needs of persons with ID. It happens because of the underestimation of their learning potential and capacity. The parents have to go through an enormous struggle, facing multiple problems at every stage of life, including worry about the big question of 'what after us?'

Mainstreaming a person with ID is the biggest challenge. One important area in this regard is vocational rehabilitation. This cannot be done individually by parents. They need to join hands and start supported employment centres where adults with ID can be trained and employed. Some of the higher-functioning adults can also be employed in mainstream jobs under proper supervision and with required adaptations.

It is ironic that for a population of 15,05,624 there are only 557 NGOs working all over the country to serve the needs of people with four severe disabilities—intellectual disability, autism, cerebral palsy, and multiple disabilities. Even if we take a liberal estimate of 100 persons with disabilities per NGO, it will mean only 55,000 are getting any kind of services. They hardly get any professional support in addressing training needs, and employment is a far cry.

The concerned government departments still do not have credible statistical data. This speaks of the lack of sincere efforts in planning as well as implementation of schemes and programmes. Such departments must have a good component of professionals who have the knowledge and experience enabling them to understand the needs of the sector and make planned interventions.

Right to Equal Opportunity

The UNCRPD holds the potential to create a humane world where society is obligated to provide opportunities and conditions for fulfilling human rights for all. It is important to note that the comprehensive list of general principles mentioned in Article 3 of the UNCRPD has emerged from debates and discussions among people with various types of disabilities and families.

General principles are at the core of the Human Rights Treaty, and they form the spirit of the UNCRPD. These principles represent the essential humanness of people with disabilities and can serve as a foundation for changes in legislation, policy, and practice. The Rights of Persons with Disabilities Act, formulated by India in December 2016, has adopted all the general principles of the UNCRPD. The real challenge lies ahead in its implementation in letter and spirit. People with disabilities have been neglected for far too long in India, largely considered a family responsibility and not the State's duty. The dominant approach has been a charity attitude, and this must change. Equal opportunities and required facilities alone will bring about a change. Breaking myths about disability, accessing growth opportunities such as education and employment in an inclusive environment, will dismantle notions of incapacity and slowly substitute them with a diversity approach. It does not need huge finances; it demands changes in mindsets.

General Principles in UNCRPD

- Respect for inherent dignity, individual autonomy including the freedom to make one's own choices, and independence of persons
- Non-discrimination
- Full and effective participation and inclusion in society
- Respect for difference and acceptance of persons with disabilities as part of human diversity and humanity
- Equality of opportunity
- Accessibility
- Equality between men and women
- Respect for the evolving capacities of children with disabilities and respect for the right of children with disabilities to preserve their identities

The state is duty-bound to provide equal opportunities for health, education, accessible infrastructure, and employment to all its citizens. Similarly, society owes the responsibility to dismantle unfair and unjust attitudes, such as assumptions of incapacity, seeing disability as a curse, non-recognition of growth needs like education and employment, as well as basic human needs like nutrition, health, and safe living.

The World Bank report commissioned by MSJE highlights the poor state of affairs of people with disabilities. Poor implementation of commitments by the government continues despite creating a separate department in 2011 for the empowerment of people with disabilities. According to the report, 'India's implementation capacity is generally weak in a number of areas of service delivery, which are most critical to improving the situation of disabled people.'* It is distressing to witness the immense hardships of parents and families and their children with ID. Over the last decade, very few parents have come forward to start such services, which is understandable. With increasing competition and struggles, people are left with little time and energy to take up voluntary service, which alone has brought the services we see today. There is enough experience to undertake realistic planning and execution at a large scale, but it can only happen with government support. Muskaan and a few other NGOs have created good service models for adult training and employment, as well as safe living options. This is not charity; it is simply honouring the rights of every human being by providing equal opportunities for living a life of respect and dignity.

* https://documents1.worldbank.org/curated/en/577801468259486686/pdf/502090WP0Peopl1Box0342042B01PUBLIC1.pdf

11

Muskaan: An Incredible Journey

Muskaan's journey is also my personal journey in life. I don't feel like segregating the two because sometimes life-transforming situations and their demands on us change us in unimaginable ways. Muskaan and I have grown together. What follows in this chapter are glimpses into a human journey. In pursuit of our goals and aspirations, human experiences often get eclipsed, whereas it is these experiences alone that drive us on our path in life's journey; it is our learnings and insights that are our real gains.

Today, after 40 years, when I think of Muskaan, the first feeling that comes to my mind is, 'How did it happen?' The whole journey looks amazing. I did not start with any ambition or plan; it wasn't clear as to what could happen or how it would happen. The one and only thought was that my son, Puneet, had taught me so much about nurturing the growth of a person with intellectual disability, and I owe it to share my learning experiences with other children and their families. Seeing the abysmal situation regarding services in this sector, I felt I must work to create opportunities so that they can live a decent and respectful life. Their disability was not on my mind. I only thought of them as children and adults who, like everyone else, have an inherent drive to live with enthusiasm and fullness.

Today, I feel as if whatever incidents happened in my life, my learnings, my perspectives about life, and the choices I was making, were taking me in one direction—the creation of Muskaan. I was intrigued by the workings of the mind in a person with limited intellect, where some of the higher intellectual functions were not optimally developed as in others. I was also interested in understanding how such a person would perceive and understand the world. As I involved myself in connecting with many other persons with varied disabilities, a deep appreciation and respect grew in me to understand their world. They were heroes in my life who inspired me to work as much as I could to enhance their lives. My friends, professor Anita Ghai and Sri Javed Abidi, who were wheelchair users, greatly influenced me by their strength and determination. They increased my sensitivity manifold about the lack of facilities that are faced by people with disabilities.

Puneet at home and the young adults at Muskaan gave me many opportunities to observe and understand their minds, behaviours, aspirations, and feelings. I found, except for higher intellectual functions, the rest of the mind's functions, such as feelings and psychological needs, were functioning exactly like those of any other person. I understood the centrality of emotional well-being in a person's life and its effects on learning, performance, and behaviour. I could see the injustice being done to them by the non-recognition of their psycho-social needs and the absence of good learning and growth opportunities. Muskaan became a platform where we could address many of their important needs through skill-building and growth-oriented programmes, such as life skills, cognitive enrichment, recreation, sports, performing arts, friendship building, and inclusive social situations. I, along with the

Muskaan team of teachers, continued designing such training programmes and saw good results of focused training efforts with our students.

Two guiding lights in my life have been people with intellectual disability and my deep concern with existential questions in life, which led me to study Vedanta and other spiritual traditions—a profound knowledge system that transforms the way we think about ourselves, others, and the world. I gradually realised that our world is constructed by our minds and no two minds are the same. This means each of us carries a diversity of world views, which is authentic and must be respected for what it is. Life is a gift, and everyone enjoys it in their own unique way. We are all a part of a larger order, not knowing why we are here yet continue to judge everyone on some imagined criteria. What ultimately matters is that everyone should be treated with love and respect and given the opportunity for a full life as much as possible. The young people with intellectual disabilities brought a huge shift in my perception of disability, from deficiency to diversity, from a judgmental attitude to respectful acceptance, and from arrogance to an attitude of humility.

Each day on this journey was taken as it came, often with new demands and challenges. I had already been trained by my son, Puneet, who has Down Syndrome, to shift my focus from problems to solution-oriented thinking, and my mind was tuned to explore the ways to deal with challenges. I unhesitatingly asked for advice and support from people who could be trusted for their sensitivity and maturity. I was careful about my conversations with people so that others would not get the impression that I was either seeking their sympathy or boasting about whatever little I was doing. It taught me an attitude of humility in all my interactions with people. I also reminded myself very clearly that I may not always receive a positive response from people, and I don't have to feel bad or offended by it. I was increasingly and firmly rooted in the cause of Muskaan, overcoming ego-centric needs, and that was the need of the hour. Social injustice to so many lives, without any fault of their own, was too much for me to bear, so every step in this direction was an answer to the call of my conscience.

Connecting with Parents and Professionals

Muskaan was registered as a society in 1982. From the beginning, we knew that the work in this area could only be successfully done when parents, families, and professionals join hands with each other. It was widely known that unless parents united to make it happen, the services wouldn't be established. This led to naming the society as 'Parents Association'. It is a different matter that with the growth of the NGO, the role of the parents keeps changing. It becomes increasingly difficult for the parents to shoulder the responsibility that an organisation demands because it needs skills, professional background and lot of time and energy.

Though there are ample career opportunities for professionals in this field, experience has shown that most of such programmes addressing diverse needs of this sector have been initiated by parents themselves. Creating and sustaining such services involves struggles at every step of the way, including finding good teachers and dedicated professionals, development of infrastructure, raising money to create and sustain services, and cultivating an ethos of interpersonal sensitivity and spirit of service. It necessitates partnership between parents and professionals in building a culture, which is the backbone of organisations like Muskaan.

In the early years, support of other parents and caring professionals, mainly the doctors of genetics department of AIIMS, was very critical. It brought a kind of confidence and handholding that was needed in the initial years. Meeting with Dr I. C. Verma, a pioneer in genetics in India, was a significant event in the birth of Muskaan. His kindness, generosity, and expertise in the field gave me and other parents, connected at that time, great strength and confidence to move on our path in creating needed services for children and adults with ID and their families. For almost a decade, we used his office as our meeting place, using AIIMS lecture halls and auditorium for many activities of the Association. His team of doctors was always willing to help us with whatever we needed. Dr Verma and his department stood like a rock behind us in the early years of Muskaan.

In hindsight, I realise that it was not any ambition that resulted in today's Muskaan. The call of conscience was so strong that it was not letting me rest. Deep reverence for life and distress at social injustice were the driving force. I felt deeply disturbed by the discriminatory attitudes towards certain sections of humanity, and it appeared totally irrational to me. I had always been very sensitive to others' problems, and something within me was telling me that if 'you really mean it, then do something to make life better for others.' I had learnt a lot by working with my son and many other children and saw the importance of focused training in enhancing many skills needed for everyday living. Traditionally, Indian society had ignored the need for providing training to such children and accepted them as they were, sometimes out of compassion, sympathy, or pity and often getting amused by their awkward, 'funny', and simple ways. Assumption of incapacity was dominant, and training efforts depended on the mindset of the individual family.

The prevailing attitudes of hopelessness were not acceptable to me. I was keen to apply my learnings with other students of Muskaan. I, along with teachers, designed appropriate training programmes that could address their growth needs. My subject, Psychology, taught me how to simplify learning situations and the significance of strengthening their cognitive and other mental functions. We had no model to follow, no chartered path to walk on. It meant doing small experiments with minimal resources and carving out a plan and programme, aiming at capacity building of children and adults with ID. My son was born in 1976, and he was barely 6 years old when Muskaan started. I was still grappling with my personal challenges of mothering a child with Down Syndrome, commitments to my family, my passion for teaching psychology to young students at Lady Sri Ram College, as well as the fledgling organisation that Muskaan was in its initial years. God has been very kind to place me in a family that always supported me in all my pursuits.

Understanding the Training Needs— A Creative Journey with the Students

Muskaan, the name of our society, defined our approach. I vividly remember the day when, in one of our executive meetings, we were trying to choose a name for our newly launched vocational training centre. We did not like a name that was condescending in its meaning. We wanted a forward-looking and happy name, choosing 'Muskaan'. Years later, we came to realise that it was the perfect name, as individuals with intellectual disabilities possess a unique capability to spread love and joy to those around them.

Muskaan charted its own path in developing training programmes for adults with intellectual disabilities. We made a conscious choice of working with adults aged 16 and above, as nothing existed for them at that time. There was a dearth of teachers in the 80s and 90s, and we still find it difficult to get competent teachers. Special educators are not well-prepared to work with adults with special needs because teachers' training courses lack the focus on psychological understanding of persons with ID. In such a situation, we needed to enhance the knowledge base of the teachers and work on their capacity building so that they could understand the mind functions of an individual with intellectual disabilities and appreciate their mental space, making their teaching more effective.

Training people with intellectual disabilities demands creative ways to reach out to them to make learning effective. Every teacher knows well that education and teaching-learning itself is a creative process, especially so when the student has problems in learning. Working with students at Muskaan and my son at home brought immense depth to my understanding of their mind and its functions. When we think of a person, we often fail to recognise the multidimensionality of the inner world. Indian psychology (psychology in Indian spiritual traditions) identifies four aspects of the inner world:

Manas—mind with its needs and desires

Buddhi—faculty of cognition, capable of understanding everything from the simple to the complex, from the concrete to the abstract

Chitta—impressions created by past experiences

Ahankar—ego, the integrating centre within, which we refer to as 'I'

Like everyone else, people with cognitive or intellectual disabilities share all these dimensions, except that intellect is not optimally developed. Psychology further analyses intellect and the process of knowing and understanding into seven cognitive functions, namely attention, perception, memory, concept formation, thinking, reasoning, and problem-solving. Intellectual disability occurs due to the suboptimal development of these cognitive functions, affecting overall cognition. Strengthening these functions through a variety of learning experiences or training enhances cognitive capacities. People with intellectual disabilities are quite good at concrete thinking, though they have difficulty in abstract thinking. This limits the scope of academic learning. Their ability for concrete thinking enables them to learn and perform concrete operations involved in everyday life, including the making of simple products and performing tasks that do not require complex judgment or reasoning.

At Muskaan, we never diluted our focus on capacity building for individuals with intellectual disabilities. With experience and practical research, our training programmes grew in quality and depth. Periodical reviews helped make the programmes and activities more relevant to the needs of the students. This resulted in twofold growth of our training programmes:

1) Vocational and work-related training
2) Life skills or personal growth-oriented programmes

The latter included training activities for cognitive enhancement, social-emotional understanding, self-regulation, discipline, and independence in daily life, and knowledge and awareness of the self and physical and social environment. Thus, both kinds of training programmes aimed to contribute to a fuller life. These areas are important for every person, but more so for people with intellectual disabilities. In other children, we assume that with general exposure to varied life situations, they will learn and grow in these areas. However, people with ID require help in developing these skills. We need to go back to basics of all these skills and then choose simple ways to facilitate their learning. All such interventions require a humanistic perspective, and one needs to shift from a utilitarian approach. The humanistic perspective promotes a person-centric approach where everyone is valued, irrespective of their level of achievement and ability. It contributes to the emotional well-being of a person. Muskaan's experience has shown that everyone can learn and be involved in productive work according to their ability. This approach and attitude have a transforming impact on teachers as well as students. Students at Muskaan have humanised the whole environment, promoting respect and acceptance of everyone regardless of ability, achievements, and social hierarchies. It has facilitated team spirit, congenial work environment, cooperative efforts, openness in dialogue, caring relationships, and ownership of roles and responsibilities.

Our students kept driving us to find solutions to every challenge. It was thrilling to walk on the path of mind-building, which raised several fundamental questions related to the human mind and intellect. I realised that psychology as a discipline had limited understanding of the mind of individuals with ID. It inspired my imagination and encouraged me to explore the world of a person whose cognitive faculties were not optimally developed. There is a huge potential for research in this field that can enhance overall understanding of the human mind.

Working with the students demanded a lot of perseverance, patience, and continued efforts in building their knowledge and skills. It is not a simple task. One needed to find creative ways to reach out to them. It required a great deal of discussion with teachers to build a deeper understanding of the challenges that students with ID face and the use of appropriate methods and strategies for facilitating their learning in several areas of life. It needed personalised efforts on the part of teachers for every individual student.

There were no adult training programmes when we started our vocational and life skills training centre for adults with intellectual disability in 1989. Muskaan built its own curriculum, learning activities, pedagogy, and learning material. We devised assessment methods to record progression in learning. A constant effort has been made over the last three decades to improve our training programmes, and it will continue in the future with development of our understanding of the cognitive and personality functions as well as learning potential in adults with intellectual disability. In some ways, it is an ongoing research programme that helps understand the ways in which the human mind functions when there is compromised intellect with intact emotions, aspirations, and psychological needs.

Every project of Muskaan was developed to address the needs of our students and their families, resulting in four main projects:

- Vocational and life skills training and employment of adults with intellectual disability
- Assisted living facility for senior adults, as their parents were getting old and were worried about the safety of their wards
- Family support services
- Awareness and advocacy

Work in all the above areas aimed at providing growth opportunities to persons with intellectual disabilities. Families with a member with intellectual disability need support services, guidance, knowledge, and emotional support to be able to meet multiple challenges. Similarly, an accepting and inclusive society needs to address the needs of all and be free from prejudices; it needs the right kind of information, understanding, and awareness.

Assisted Living Facility—An Answer to 'Who After Us?'

Looking back in time, I wonder how I gathered the courage to initiate this project. Creating a residential facility for adults with intellectual disabilities meant immense responsibility for the whole lifespan, including old age and sickness. Debating it for almost a year in the executive board, thrashing out all doubts, apprehensions, and uncertainties, we resolved to start this project in 2012. By then, I had seen how Muskaan had tackled so many challenges in the past. It gave me the courage and confidence to initiate this much needed project. All of us at Muskaan had no experience of the demands of such a project. However, the only dominant thought was, 'if not us, who else will do it?' Single or senior-aged parents were coming to meet me, requesting to do something for the long-term security and safe living of their wards so that they could die in peace. It had to be a group effort, and that, too, by parents' initiative, as is the experience all over India, and in other countries as well. Securing necessary services could come only through a parents' efforts.

Our experience of working and understanding the adult men and women with ID had convinced us that their needs are no different from any other person of that age. However, we needed to have an in-depth understanding of each resident and their family to enable us to understand their behaviours patters and facilitate group living. We were clear that our assisted living facility should run like a family away from their own homes, where everyone is involved in maintaining their small rooms and common areas with assigned roles and responsibilities and should be able to make choices regarding their likes and interests. A fair degree of autonomy, responsible roles, structure and discipline, and privacy are the hallmarks of adult life and that was central to our planning along with nutrition, hygiene, work, and recreation. The biggest source of confidence came from our students because they always rose to the occasion and never failed us in any of the programmes designed for them. We finally started the project with 6 residents—4 men and 2 women—with faith that we will be able to handle the difficulties as they come.

Muskaan confirmed my faith time and again that honest, sincere, and focused work brings results. With support from the National Trust, a community centre with three acres of land in Dera Village, part of South Delhi, was given to

Muskaan for running an assisted living facility. A community of friends and relatives of residents and other team members donated generously to make the building habitable with good infrastructure including greening of the surrounding land. A new team was built under the leadership of a newly appointed professional to establish this project. She herself had a daughter with multiple disabilities. Intensive work with residents required much more staff, escalating the salary expenditure. Funds were collected through generous donations by large-hearted people in the community because it would have been a huge expense on the part of parents to fully fund the regular expenses. Constant support by the executive board, National Trust, and parents of residents, led to a successful creation of an assisted living facility for 20 adult men and women. Our vision was to create a home away from home where residents could participate in its running as per their abilities. Residents were encouraged to decide about the food choices, outings, celebrations, games, sports, and other recreational activities. They were going to Muskaan for vocational training and employment. Residents went home for short vacations as connection with their families was seen to be important for their emotional well-being. The entire residential complex became so attractive that the villagers of Dera started demanding their community centre back for their own use. Delhi government buckled under their pressure and did not extend the lease beyond April 2021. We needed to shift the entire facility somewhere else. Renting 2–3 apartments meant huge rents. We decided to build the facility on our own premises at Muskaan. Muskaan friends, caring individuals, and organisational donors, again, provided huge support in raising funds of three crores and that made it possible to build an additional 400 sq m area as per the government norms. All this happened during the pandemic between 2019 to 2021. Our residents shifted to this new facility in January 2021.

Uncommon Challenges

If Puneet forced me to question unhelpful attitudes in many areas of life, including underestimation of their capacities, Muskaan forced me to examine my own conduct. I could not have expected other people in the community to change their attitudes unless I myself was changed deep within. I had to bridge the gap between thoughts and deeds, my role at Muskaan demanded that I should stand true to my ideals. I could not have expected other team members to follow what I myself did not show in my behaviour and conduct. Claim to recognition had to be completely abandoned because it vitiates the team spirit and social environment. The truth is that collective efforts alone bring results when it comes to a social cause. It had already dawned on me that many common pursuits that we undertake in everyday living lead us nowhere. They put us into a vicious cycle of wanting more and more to fulfil our own needs and aspirations. The need for name and fame is another trap that can misdirect one's thoughts and deeds and deprive one of the real gains in life—emotional and spiritual growth. Moreover, gratitude was becoming my way of responding to the world around me. Our children have such a feeling of camaraderie that they teach us lessons in cooperation and care rather than competing with others. They may feel unhappy if one ignores or neglects them, but they don't get hurt if someone excels.

My study of Vedanta strengthened my resolve to always follow truth and never compromise the value system. It became a sort of adventure in life, dealing with various demands with a sense of duty and commitment. It precludes pretensions that are encouraged by personal and social situations to gain short-term results. It encourages objectivity and a scientific approach. It makes one see through the tricks that the mind keeps playing and entangling us in the futile pursuits of life. It demands that things need to be seen as they are, rather than what we would like them to be. It demands growing out of egocentrism, which pushes us towards coloured perception to suit our needs. Pursuing a larger cause demands transcending narrow self-interest and concerns. The more one can do that, the more it attracts people to join and support the mission. This kind of honesty within oneself becomes a source of conviction and courage. It enables one to become transparent in thought and action. Being authentic requires inner strength and maturity.

Humanistic Approach to Management

I knew only one way of doing things—keeping focus on the larger mission as well as caring for people who were working as part of the team. Nothing can be achieved alone unless one is supported by a team of people. Care and respect form the foundation of such a team. I wished to see smiling and healthy people around. I also knew that there is a fundamental need in every person to feel loved and cared for, and one enjoys the trust that others place in them. For me, the means to achieve a goal were as important as the goal itself. If we can respect and value everyone, it brings forth positive energy that lies within everyone. Compassionate understanding is an expression of love, respect, and trust. This is a universal principle of human psychology.

Muskaan's work needed empathy and service orientation. It is much easier to teach skills and impart knowledge, but empathy and service orientation required a change in attitude that are hard to build though it can be encouraged and facilitated. Thus, those who chose to work with Muskaan and continued with it had already, in some measure, ensured these qualities in themselves. The challenge was to sustain and encourage it, and demonstrate it in one's conduct, daily interactions, and decisions. One cannot expect from others without exemplifying it in one's own thoughts and actions.

Practical demands of implementing programmes and activities through skilled teachers and other team members and developing a team of caring staff members required a delicate balance of emphasis on quality and non-acceptance of unhelpful attitude and behaviour from team members. Neither could there be a compromise in the quality of work with students, nor could one overlook the unhelpful attitudes that some team members may have. It meant a personal connect with every member of the team, understanding their needs and sensitivities, recognising their vulnerabilities, and finding ways to make them feel empowered and valued.

Human-centric management is the biggest challenge of organisations like Muskaan that are working with people who need extra sensitivity and understanding. Keeping alive that spirit is a big challenge, and it needs a humanised environment. The whole team, including teachers, management, and other team members, are constantly exposed to humanising experiences while working with the students who always emanate love, care, happiness, and respect.

The management team needed to have a fine balance between task orientation and a people-oriented attitude and approach. I have intrinsic faith in people. I always start with trust in my relationship with people, though keeping needed cautions in mind regarding human vulnerabilities. Most of the time, I never felt the urgency for instant corrections or harsh measures. I believed in the inherent human tendency to be good and felt that its expression needed a certain kind of environment of acceptance, self-correction, and self-improvement. Dishonesty, cheating, and lies had no place where everyone was engaged in improving lives of others. Creating conditions that are conducive to self-introspection are far superior to other ways in bringing long term changes in oneself and others.

I also thought that people are sacrosanct; their psychological needs and feelings matter much more than anything else. A caring attitude towards others not only strengthens but also improves everyone's life, including your own. Our children give us immense opportunities to learn the value of human-centric approach and make a shift from ego-centric to human-centric attitude.

Meeting Wonderful People

As far back as I can remember, I never had negative experiences with people. Or it may be that these did not register strongly in my mind. Many people were willing to support the cause directly or indirectly. Muskaan started to build its own circle of friends including school and college students, volunteers, parents, and donors. They gave us a lot of optimism to carry on with our goal of establishing required services and growth opportunities for persons with ID. Being a mother helped in developing trust with new acquaintances. I have seen so much positivity in people that it became an overwhelming experience and impacted my overall attitude towards others. It taught me the perils of a judgmental attitude towards others. Whenever I met someone to seek support, I used to prepare myself for insensitive comments or attitudes. Though I rarely came across that, it helped me to insulate myself from disappointments as I told myself that if people were helpful, that is Muskaan's gain, and if not, then why should I expect everyone to feel for the cause that I value so much?

I remember how our friends and architects persuaded Mr Ahluwalia, one of the top builders of Delhi, to agree to take up construction of the Muskaan building at Vasant Kunj. The building is appreciated by all for its design and quality of construction. Top professionals of Delhi took up various specialised aspects of building, e.g., design of the building, designing electrical and plumbing systems, landscape, structural design, etc., without any charge. Several officers from Delhi Development Authority (DDA) and other concerned departments helped in getting required clearances. The list appears to be endless.

Raising an amount of two crores for the building in 2001 was a huge task. The first major funding of 35 lacs came from the Japan Embassy. Friends and relatives in the USA raised almost 1/3 of the total building cost. Many people gave donations in the name of their parents and family members. Muskaan needed funds not only for creating infrastructure but also running its programmes that involved a substantial amount of recurring expenses. Crowdsourcing has been our main source of funding Muskaan projects with occasional bigger donations from corporate and individual donors. Ever since we entered our new building, a new set of requirements came up as it was another phase of Muskaan's growth. Many parents and professionals who were intimately connected with Muskaan had put in a lot of effort not only in raising financial resources but also knowledge base for managing a growing organisation.

It is amazing to see so many people who helped without seeking any recognition. There have been many more people who selflessly gave their time and expertise to get Muskaan where it stands today. I have an overwhelming sense of gratitude for everyone; I can't imagine Muskaan without them.

Leadership and its Challenges

Building an organisation that always remains tuned to its mission with focused efforts demanded full-time engagement, 24x7 involvement. Life became an experiment, and Muskaan became my *karmabhumi*, creating challenges at every step of the way. All decisions and responses had to be carefully chosen. The foundational values were very clear in my mind. I was inimical to a hierarchical attitude and believed in the wisdom of every person. I understood that a strong team necessitates recognition of collective wisdom and complementary efforts. Participatory discussion and decision-making brought collective wisdom to resolving the issues, and it proved to be very helpful, allowing team members to accept decisions more readily. It is important to recognise and appreciate the interdependent nature of human society; team spirit brings so much wisdom and effort to any endeavour. Asking for support became natural because no one can claim perfection in life. Differences of opinion pushed for greater clarity in thinking. Having a sense of gratitude for everyone's contribution started showing in a caring and focused team and its work. The leaders need to be very clear in their thought process so that the rationale could be shared for every decision and action. Willingness to accept one's limitations or mistakes gives an extra push to respectful relationships.

Building and sustaining the ethos and culture of an organisation, particularly an NGO, is paramount. Its foundational values are important for moving towards its mission. Gandhiji's famous saying that whenever taking any policy decision, think of the last person in the social hierarchy who will get affected became our guiding principle. Every decision had to be evaluated for its contribution towards enriching the lives of persons with intellectual disabilities and their families. The well-being of the members of Muskaan team always remained central without crossing boundaries unnecessarily.

Advocacy for Rights

Being a part of the larger disability sector was important to advocate for the rights of people with ID. I personally learnt a lot under the leadership of the late Mr Javed Abidi, who was a dynamic leader and held a powerful voice within the sector of people with disabilities. His political acumen made him a good interlocutor with the government. During this time, I met many inspiring heroes who worked with limited resources all their lives and raised a voice for the rights of people with different disabilities. Many of these people themselves had various disabilities, and they changed my notions about people with disabilities. I saw that their challenge was not their disability but the lack of growth opportunities to live a full life like every other citizen. I realised the tyranny of misconceptions and prejudices of the larger society. By and large, society thought that the impoverishment of their lives arose from their disability, whereas the truth is that it was the lack of needed facilities, which was the limiting factor. Thus, as I got more and more familiar with the lives of so many people with disabilities, my resolve to counter social injustice to people with intellectual disabilities grew stronger and we at Muskaan kept making efforts to enrich their lives through creating growth opportunities for them.

It is a common observation all over the world that social awakening for the rights of people with disabilities came up only when they themselves raised a voice against the discriminatory attitude of society. In the case of people with severe disabilities, parents and families became their voice, giving rise to the parents' movement.

The entire journey has been a wonderful saga of beautiful and deep insights and learnings, some of which I want to share with the readers:

1. It is possible to be happy without putting any conditions to it. We lose so much in life by pondering over what we do not have.
2. The true meaning of reverence lies in accepting and respecting all forms of creation—plants, animals, or humans; a part of the larger mysterious order of the universe including us.
3. Unconditional and selfless love is difficult, but it enriches both the giver and receiver. The more we can cultivate selfless love and care for others, compassion becomes a way of responding to the world.

4. The cultivation of a valuable attitude of patience for everyone made life much easier and peaceful; it helped in facing many difficult situations in life.
5. We waste so much energy seeking our own glory and forget that it is an emotional need for everyone. Recognising this helps build understanding and sensitivity for others.
6. Every difficult situation in life has the potential to make us more mature and stronger. The key lies in our response to the challenge.
7. Life is simple and beautiful when we avoid creating unnecessary complications.
8. In the humdrum of life, we often forget to celebrate the simple joys.
9. Learning to stay focused on what one believes is right, regardless of praise or criticism from others.

12

Vedanta: My Guiding Force in Life

I have been an ardent student of Vedanta and feel blessed for getting exposure to it by superb teachers of Vedanta. I bow down to them with immense gratitude for giving direction to my life, which I was desperately seeking. They set an example that inspired my approach to teaching and later my role in steering the growth of Muskaan and its services. It established an overall framework that guided my perspective in understanding and dealing with my roles and responsibilities, interpersonal relationships, and various challenges that life keeps throwing at us.

Adversities in life play a dual role. They rattle us, but they also open doors for new learnings. Circumstances that life puts us in are not within our control, but we have options regarding our response to them. There is a human tendency to react rather than respond appropriately to deal with adverse life situations and their challenges. Reaction is propelled by subconscious or unconscious forces deeply rooted in our emotional experiences and needs. They are often counterproductive and happen automatically without conscious control. Such subjective projections prevent us from taking an objective view of life situations. The study of Vedanta made me see the trappings of the mind that continuously keep us on a warpath with ourselves and the world. We become so immersed in the problems that we forget to look for solutions. We start blaming others or our circumstances and keep brooding over the difficulties and finding catharsis in the thought 'Why Me?' Such a mental state requires reorientation of our thinking. Just as we exclaim 'Why Me', we can also say 'Why Not Me?' We need to question our emotional reactions because they do not help in dealing with the situations and rather aggravate our difficulties and cause suffering. It also affects clarity and objectivity in thinking. We need to understand the root causes of our suffering and work to eliminate them. It can enhance our strength and maturity, making us capable of dealing with the challenges of life. It reduces our vulnerability to hurts and grief and helps us to overcome them. It encourages a solution-oriented approach in the face of difficulties. It has the potential to teach us some valuable lessons of life which may enhance our effectiveness in coping with challenging situations. Thus, adversities can become a huge learning ground enabling us to grow within and attain stability, inner strength, and inner calmness.

During this spiritual journey, I found that Muskaan slowly became a mission in my life. I experienced a different picture of the world through the eyes of young people with ID. I saw so much love, joy, innocence, and purity in their being, which made me question my own attitudes and misconceptions of society towards them. I could see how social conditionings had created havoc in my own acceptance of my little baby. It was a painful realisation that our distorted ways of thinking and judging could impoverish so many lives. What right do we have to marginalise others who, like us, have a chance to experience an amazingly beautiful world? A churning within gradually started expanding the boundaries of my consciousness.

I saw a kind of divinity in the children with whom I was working at Muskaan, and every one of them had been dear to me for what they were. They all became a source of my inspiration to work as much as possible towards enriching their lives. Their right to a respectful life was denied to them by the prejudiced notions of society.

A journey from my personal pain to a larger cause has been amazing in terms of opening the mind and expanding consciousness. These were significant transformations in life initiated and sustained by my study of Vedanta and other spiritual knowledge systems of India.

Pursuit of Existential Inquiry and Vedanta

Existential questions have always captivated my interest and curiosity. From an early age of 4–5 years, I used to be fascinated by the stars, sun, and moon in the sky. I distinctly recall visiting a temple with my mother, where I was mesmerised by the semi-formed stone idols of gods and goddesses. It sparked a deep desire within me to see and connect with the divine which continued later also. I eagerly embraced rituals, fasting on auspicious days, and reading religious texts like the Ramayana, all in the hope of having a glimpse of the divine. These experiences occurred before the dawn of logic and reasoning in my mind as I entered my teen years in the adolescent phase.

My father was a thinker with a saintly temperament, and he often engaged me in discussions about social and religious issues. His influence steered my thoughts towards deeper existential questions. As I grew up in my teen ages, I found interest in philosophy, immersing myself in the works of great thinkers like Sarvapalli Radhakrishnan and Professor S.

N. Dasgupta. Though I may be hardly comprehending their ideas at such a young age, but it intensified my quest for existential questions.

Choosing psychology as a subject in school stemmed from my fascination with the complexities of the human mind and behaviour. With an inherently introspective temperament, self-reflection came naturally to me. I always approached life with an intellectual curiosity, analysing everything through a rational lens. While I distanced myself from outward religious practices, but the desire to know and see God persisted. Psychology itself could not provide satisfactory answers to my existential questions. It wasn't until my late 20s, when I listened to lectures on the Bhagavad Gita by revered Vedanta teacher Swami Chinmayananda, that I felt a sense of direction to my search. Listening to the teachings of Swami Dayananda Saraswati opened a whole new wealth of knowledge about Advaita Vedanta.

Contrary to popular belief, Indian scriptures demand an analytical and rational approach to life's complexities. Vedanta, often referred to as the science of life, delves deep into profound knowledge about the self and the universe. Its central inquiry revolves around the fundamental question: 'Who am I?'. This inquiry led me to a profound realisation about the superficial notions of selfhood that one finds in mainstream psychology. It provided me a direction to deal with my inner struggles arising from various situations in life. Two such prominent struggles in my life centered around dealing with my own emotions with regard to the disability of my son and nurturing the growth of Muskaan and its services. Both meant changes in attitudes, social conditionings, objectivity, and moving away from ego-centric thinking to issue-based resolutions. My spiritual journey, guided by Vedanta, yoga, and Buddhism, has been deeply transformative. It showed that the root cause of most problems in life is our ego-centric perspective. Understanding the oneness in all enhanced my capacity for empathy and reverence for all. A recognition of human suffering and the ephemeral nature of worldly pursuits broadens one's perspective, fosters objectivity, and cultivates compassion and inner peace. Vedanta declares that true fulfillment and lasting peace can only be found by transcending the ego-centric perspective and uncovering the deeper reality of the self known as atman.

Central Inquiry in Vedanta

Vedanta, known as *adhyatma vidya*, may rightfully be termed the science of life. Its intricate analysis of human mind and tendencies addresses every conceivable question that may arise in a seeker's mind. It encompasses profound knowledge systems that explore the true nature of self and the universe. The name 'Vedanta' derives from the knowledge presented in the concluding portion of the Vedas, namely the Upanishads. Central to Vedanta is the inquiry into understanding the true nature of the self, called *adhyatmavidya*, encapsulated in the question, 'Who am I?' A deep analysis of this question unveils a remarkable vision of humanity and its world, one that diverges significantly from empirical notions of the Self and universe. Vedanta elucidates the non-self character of body, mind, intellect, and ego—entities universally perceived as the self or 'I', including mainstream psychology. As Sri Radhakrishnan eloquently stated:

> The body, the sense organs, the mind and the ego all lay claim to being the self of man. Before inquiry man takes one or the other of them as self. But the philosophical inquiry reveals their non-self character. It reveals each one of them as object and not the subject, each is a *sanghata* or aggregate in the terminology of Buddha, and as such, subject to change and destruction.

Through meticulous analysis supported by profound logic in Vedanta, we come to realise that our conception of 'I' or 'Me' is largely comprised of 'self-images' or 'self-notions'. These self-images are formed early in life and influence the way we perceive ourselves and others. They are shaped by our own perceptions and the reflected appraisals from others. Subconsciously, we strive to defend these images, although such efforts often prove futile, akin to chasing clouds.

All spiritual traditions in India begin with the analysis of human life conditions, its ephemerality, upheavals, and sufferings. Its goal is liberation from human suffering. It reveals that the unending pursuit of happiness in wealth, name, and fame etc. might bring a temporary release from a sense of inadequacy and insufficiency, but it could never lead to a lasting fulfilment, peace, and happiness.

These knowledge systems emphatically declare that the only solution to this vicious web of pleasures and pains lies in tracing them to the tendencies of inner workings of mind and in the unfolding of deeper reality/truth that alone can emancipate one from the pulls and pushes of life.

Understanding the true nature of self or I and the world brings a paradigm shift in ways of thinking about oneself and our world. Vedanta declares that our true identity transcends these self-notions. It is called atman. Its nature is defined as *sat, chit, anantam* (existence, knowledge/consciousness, eternal, and ever full respectively). It is the basis of all creations/ manifestations including space and time. It is in consonance with our experience. 'I' including everyone's experience of 'I' is the subject or knower to whom the universe presents itself as the object of knowledge. Vedanta provides superb logic to make it evident through the following analytical methods:

- Subject-object analysis (*Drik-Drishya-Viveka)*
- Analysis of three states of being—waking, dreaming, and sleeping (from the Mandukya Upanishad)

What is this 'I' that we consistently experience within ourselves as feeler, thinker, seer, or knower? Each of us comprehends our thoughts, emotions, and perceptions, signifying that all these are known to 'me' or, in other words, 'I' am the 'knower' of these experiences. This is termed subject-object analysis, wherein one perceives oneself as the subject or I, while everything else, including the external world and internal experiences like thoughts and emotions, are objects of knowledge. Similarly, the 'I' remains unchanged—experiencer or knower, etc.—across different life stages—infancy, childhood, adolescence, adulthood, and old age. The nature of 'I' persists even amidst the three states of waking, dream, and sleep. Vedanta delves deeply into this essence of 'I or Self' and unveils astounding revelations. How everything is rooted in pure consciousness is the pinnacle of philosophical reasoning we find in *advait Vedanta.* These insights about the nature of reality have been verified repeatedly by saints, sages, and great men and women in all times from distant past to contemporary times. Some of the well-known examples are Buddha, Mahavir,

Adi Shankaracharya, Ramakrishna Paramhansa, Vivekananda, Maharshi Ramana, Shri Aurobindo, and countless other spiritual masters little known to the larger world.

Recognition of this truth fosters feeling of oneness and profound reverence for all beings. While initially it may seem strange, deep analysis of life and mind makes it look very rational and appealing. Comprehension of this thought necessitates rigorous thinking and introspection, supported by in-depth study of scriptures and commentaries on them. Moksha, the pinnacle of human perfection, reveals the limitations of ego, and offers liberation from the sense of incompleteness, facilitating a shift towards atman—a new paradigm to understand life and universe. Humanity requires this wisdom to unlock its latent potential and avert self-destruction.

Centrality of 'I' or Ego: A Case of Misplaced Identity

The focal point of our world is 'I-sense' or ego, a powerful centre that creates a world of experiences, serving largely its own needs and fancies. All its pursuits are guided by an overwhelming desire to protect, enhance, and authenticate its own experiences and viewpoints. The significance and strength of this drive emanate from the need to anchor oneself in this vast universe where we live briefly between birth and death, disappearing one day into oblivion. It is a temporary rising in an ocean of eternity.

Vedanta declares that ego or I-sense is a case of misplaced identity; it is called *dehatma-buddhi* (body-mind-sense complex—the notion that I am my body and mind). Because of this identification, whatever happens to the body and mind, happens to 'me' as well. Mind keeps playing its games throughout life. Vedanta tells us that as long as the identity is rooted in the body-mind-sense-complex, including ego, it would remain subject to upheavals of life. 'I' identified with the body-mind-sense complex (ego) would always remain incomplete, inadequate, and limited and, therefore, always in need of something more to fulfil itself. Any number of achievements are unable to quench this thirst. The ego would always remain in search of elusive fulfilment and perfection, joy and peace.

Knowledge of true self (*adhyatmvidya*) alone can counter this predicament of human beings. Vedanta declares that by constant self-inquiry and self-reflection, one needs to ascertain the true nature of I/Self as opposed to the empirical notion of self (*dehatma-buddhi*). Deep introspective analysis reveals a deceptive nature of ego and mind. Vedanta shows that self (atman) is ever full, devoid of any inadequacies or limitations. It is of the nature of pure consciousness or awareness and the source of 'I-ness' in us. Atman is explained as *Swayamjyoti*, self-evident and light of lights. It is witness to all happenings in the world including inner world of thoughts, feelings, and desires. Its veracity is proved by incontrovertible logic and reasoning and analysis of experience. That is the truth of everything, manifest or unmanifest.

Recent interest in the field of consciousness studies has brought renewed focus on consciousness by scientists and thinkers in the last two decades. Neuroscientists, physicists, mathematicians, and computer scientists are at the forefront of this research and are engaging in interesting debates over fathoming the deepest mysteries surrounding consciousness and integrating spiritual knowledge systems in their search for answers.

A Journey from Ego to Atman/Self

The shift from ego to atman is a lifetime journey that may only be initiated when our mind is ready to take this plunge. The preparation necessitates *antahkarana shuddhi* (seeing the trappings of the mind through dispassionate analysis of oneself and one's experiences) and the fourfold sadhana—*vivek*, *vairagya*, *shad sampat*, *mumukshutvam* (refer to the box). It means total deconditioning of mind enabling one to look at experiences with an open mind. *Atma-vichara* (self-analysis and self-reflection) is essential to proceed on the path of self- knowledge, as illustrated in Yoga Vasishtha:

> If one engages oneself in constant self-inquiry and sees the ever-changing nature of the world, in due time, one will attain self-knowledge . . . When the limited and conditioned feeling that I am so-and-so ceases, there arises consciousness of the all-pervading infinite.
>
> ***—Yoga Vasistha (commentary by Swami Venkatesananda, Vol 1, page 225)***

> Defects, desires, and evils do not even approach that man of wisdom whose mind is undeluded. Through wisdom (in the inner light) the entire world is clearly seen as it is; neither good fortune nor misfortune even approach one who has such clear vision. Even as the dense dark cloud that veils the sun is dispersed by wind, the darkness of ego-sense which veils the self is dispelled by wisdom (inner light). He who seeks to be established in highest state of consciousness, should

first purify his mind through cultivation of wisdom or by the kindling of the inner light, even as one desires food-grains tills the field.

—Yoga Vasistha (commentary by Swami Venkatesananda, Vol 1, page 224)

Vivek: Discrimination between transient and non-transient.

Vairagya: A sense of detachment from worldly pleasures and achievements; being objective without being overwhelmed by emotions.

Shad Sampat: The cultivation of six-fold virtues, namely:

Sama—control/discipline of mind and conduct

Dama—control/discipline of body and senses

Uparati—observance of one's duties and the elimination of that which is redundant

Titiksha—endurance of pleasure/pain; praise/criticism

Shraddha—faith in the veracity of the words of the teacher and scripture

Samadhana—deep concentration and single-minded pursuit of truth

Mumukshutvam: Earnest desire for knowledge and liberation.

Sa Vidya ya Vimuktaye (knowledge that leads to liberation) is the crowning statement of the Upanishads. It is not liberation of the 'I' but liberation from 'I-ness', the sense of individuality.

Atman=Brahman is the great equation whose meaning is unfolded in the Upanishads. It is the most profound statement that eludes our comprehension because we are rooted in ego-consciousness and transact with the world from that perspective.

Unless the mind is somewhat settled and is at peace with itself, one is not prepared enough to grasp the essence of spirituality contained in Vedantic texts. To whatever extent one can grasp, it has a monumental impact on our outlook towards life and its myriad happenings. Karma yoga and Gyan yoga are the two wings to soar higher and higher on this journey. Vedanta says that self-knowledge (*atma-gyan*) necessitates cultivation of Vivek, Vairagya, Six-fold virtues and strong urge for Moksha (liberation)

The truth of Vedanta requires rigorous pursuit of knowledge following the methods of *Shravan* (deep study of vedantic texts), *manana* (reflection on the teachings to assimilate knowledge), *nidhidhyasana (*single pointed pursuit to live life in the light of knowledge*)*. Patanjali Yogasutra has developed Ashtang Yoga and buddha's eightfold path provides a methodology towards inner purification called *antahkaran-shuddhi*.

The journey from ego to atman opens new dimensions in life. As one progresses in this journey, it changes the way one looks at oneself, others, and the world. One begins to appreciate the blessings one has in life. Everything appears full of wonders, from a small flower to huge galaxies, and one is filled with a sense of awe. All other human pursuits pale in comparison.

We live in a grand universe full of wonders and mysteries. One feels amazed at the perfect order which underlies every form of creation, be it stars, galaxies, oceans, rivers, life forms, plants, trees, etc., including human beings. The greatest wonder is the human mind itself, which is bestowed with marvellous qualities that create a whole new world—a world of ideas, a quest for knowledge, aspirations, emotions, and desires. One feels a sense of awe when one discovers that the brain, an amazingly complex creation, plays a critical role in creating a world that is outside there and the world of experience within us.

The material world as well as the psychological world are not independent of the design of sense organs and the brain. The question arises: 'Do we live in a world out there or does the world live in us?' Popper and Eccles, in the preface of their book Self and Its Brain, aptly wrote: 'When a man dies a whole universe is lost.' How did the universe come into being? What is the purpose behind it? How and why did self-conscious beings arise in this vast creation? These are the eternal questions asked by men and women of all times. They arise in everybody's mind, perhaps momentarily. Once these questions start dominating the mind space, one cannot wish them away. It would force us to look beyond everyday engagements and open a door for intense search wherever possible.

Points to Ponder

Engrossed in our own world, we seldom pause to contemplate the mysteries around us. The vast universe appears intricately designed, with billions of galaxies, solar and planetary systems operating in perfect order and harmony. It undergoes changes in meaning and complexity as the nervous system evolves, which itself is nature's most intricate creation. Additionally, the mind and consciousness, though intangible, add to the wonder of our existence. Every natural creation is unique in form, composition, beauty, and its role within the broader order of things. It's astonishing to realise that all life forms, including humans, hold diverse views of the world, each authentic in its own way. Life seems like a panorama of experiences, with each stage offering its own distinct worldview. Furthermore, we as creatures, are compelled to seek the meaning and purpose of life. Unlike other living beings, humans possess the capacity for self-reflection, which profoundly influences our lives and the world we shape.

Erwin Schrödinger, a Nobel laureate in Physics, in his book Nature of Reality, written towards the end of his life, said that 'there are two incontrovertible facts: (a) My body is a machine, (b) Its motions are under my control. The only possible inference from these two facts, I in the widest meaning of the word—that is, every conscious mind that has ever said or felt 'I'—am the person, if any, who controls the "motions of the atoms" according to the laws of nature . . . This insight itself is not new. The earliest records, to my knowledge, date back some 2,500 years or more. From the early great Upanishads, the recognition that Atman equals Brahman (the personal self equals the omnipresent, all-comprehending eternal self) was considered, far from being blasphemous, to represent the quintessence of the deepest insight into the happenings of the world.'

Afterword

Motherhood provides a valuable learning opportunity for every woman. However, raising a child who defies typical expectations is not only challenging but can lead to conflicts and anxieties that may be self-damaging. I personally faced this struggle when dealing with my child, born with Down Syndrome and intellectual disability. The journey from initial rejection to unconditional acceptance was a long and tough one but full of insights and precious learnings. He holds a unique and cherished place in my heart.

For me, he is not a person with disability. I see him as a person with a unique perspective on the world. Despite limited intellectual functions, he creates a world free from the mental constraints of complex abstract concepts. His distinctive worldview makes him a cheerful, caring, and lovable person. His innocence, simple outlook, capacity for unconditional love, and joy in life are truly touching.

I'm amazed at the power of open thinking to free us from unhealthy mental conditionings. It shows how our world is a product of our own minds. Assumptions, expectations, judgmental attitudes, and vanities prevent us from accepting realities as they are, causing unnecessary pain. Through my journey, I learnt gratitude for life's small blessings, fostering understanding and compassion.

The inspiration for writing this book stems from three main objectives. First, I wanted to share how our thinking and mental conditionings can become prisons, causing unnecessary hardships. Questioning conditioned ways of thinking can bring new perspectives towards life and calmness to the mind. Second, I felt a deep sense of injustice towards individuals with intellectual disabilities (ID), and I wanted to address the wrong notions that lead to indignity and impoverishment in their lives. Lastly, I wanted to share positive observations and experiences about individuals with ID, as we often overlook their strengths.

Muskaan's journey exemplifies how honest intentions and sincere efforts towards a just cause are rewarded by the universal order. It has strengthened my faith in the justice of the larger order within which we all operate.

ACKNOWLEDGEMENTS

My son Puneet has been my greatest teacher, challenging my misconceptions and revealing their illusory nature. This experience has led me to a more profound understanding of life, and I am immensely grateful for his presence.

I extend my heartfelt thanks to my husband and daughter, who wholeheartedly supported my endeavours. Their care and open-mindedness have allowed me to follow my path. The unwavering support and affection for Puneet from our extended family provided a significant source of strength for me. Gratitude also goes to my Muskaan family and friends from the community who joined wholeheartedly in realising our shared dreams of enhancing the lives of people with intellectual disabilities.

I enjoyed co-editing with Sonali Pawar. Initially, I was apprehensive about the clarity with which I was trying to communicate my thoughts and feelings. However, her editorial comments not only dispelled my doubts but also provided insightful suggestions that enhanced the clarity and precision of the write-up. I am grateful to Hay House for publishing the book.